Doing Anthropological Research

Doing Anthropological Research provides a practical toolkit for carrying out research. It works through the research process chapter by chapter, from the planning and proposal stage to methodologies, secondary research, ethnographic fieldwork, ethical concerns and writing strategies. Case study examples are provided throughout to illustrate the particular issues and dilemmas that may be encountered. This handy guide will be invaluable to upper-level undergraduate and postgraduate students who are studying or intending to use anthropological methods in their research.

Natalie Konopinski received her Ph.D. in Social Anthropology from the University of Edinburgh, UK, and has taught anthropological research methods to undergraduate and postgraduate students. She is currently a visiting scholar at George Mason University, USA.

Doing Anthropological Research

A practical guide

Edited by
Natalie Konopinski

Routledge
Taylor & Francis Group

LONDON AND NEW YORK

First published in 2014
by Routledge
2 Park Square, Milton Park, Abingdon, Oxon OX14 4RN

Simultaneously published in the USA and Canada
by Routledge
711 Third Avenue, New York, NY 10017

Routledge is an imprint of the Taylor & Francis Group, an informa business

British Library Cataloguing in Publication Data
A catalogue record for this book is available from the British Library

Library of Congress Cataloging in Publication Data
Doing anthropological research : a practical guide / edited by
Natalie Konopinski.
pages cm.
Includes bibliographical references and index.
1. Anthropology–Research. 2. Anthropology–Methodology. 3. Anthropology–
Fieldwork. I. Konopinski, Natalie.
GN42.D65 2013
301.072–dc23
2013001760

ISBN: 978-0-415-69754-5 (hbk)
ISBN: 978-0-415-69755-2 (pbk)
ISBN: 978-0-203-74387-4 (ebk)

Typeset in Bembo
by Taylor & Francis Books

Contents

Notes on contributors

Joost Fontein is a social anthropologist at the University of Edinburgh, UK, where he teaches the 'Imagining Anthropological Research' course upon which this book is framed. His research explores the political imbrications of landscapes, things and human substances in Zimbabwe. His Ph.D. (published in 2006) exploring the politics of heritage around Great Zimbabwe won the 2004 ASA Audrey Richards Prize. His second book *Graves & Water: Belonging, Sovereignty and the Political Materialities of Landscape* is almost complete. His third book explores the affective presence and emotive materialities of human remains. He is editor of *Journal of Southern African Studies*, founder of *Critical African Studies*, and co-founder of the Bones Collective research group.

Ian Harper is Head of Social Anthropology at the University of Edinburgh, UK. He has conducted research in South Asia in the area of medical anthropology and development, and is currently a Wellcome Trust Senior Investigator. He has taught research methods, and has extensive dissertation supervision experience at undergraduate, M.Sc. and Ph.D. levels. He was the co-founder of *Anthropology Matters* and has acted as the Ethics Officer for the Association of Social Anthropologists of the UK and Commonwealth (ASA).

John Harries is based at the University of Edinburgh, UK, and received his doctorate in Social Anthropology in 2002. He has done years of ethnographic fieldwork in Newfoundland, Canada, as well as research with health and social care professionals in the UK and has, more recently, undertaken a project concerning urban redevelopment and the industrial heritage of Edinburgh. He has extensive experience of teaching qualitative research methods at both the undergraduate and postgraduate levels and to a diverse array of audiences, from arts students, to anthropologists, to public service managers. He has also supervised many students through to the successful completion of their undergraduate and masters dissertations.

Lotte Hoek is Lecturer in Social Anthropology at the University of Edinburgh, UK. Her research interests are visual media, contemporary art and urban ethnography in South Asia. She has undertaken long-term ethnographic fieldwork in the film industry of Bangladesh. Her monograph *Cut-Pieces: Celluloid Obscenity and Popular Cinema in Bangladesh* is forthcoming from Columbia University Press.

Laura Jeffery is Lecturer in Social Anthropology at the University of Edinburgh, UK, where she has taught research methods at undergraduate and postgraduate level. She has also run qualitative methods training workshops in Ghana, Kenya, India and Pakistan for research teams working on a UK Department for International Development (DfID) Research Consortium based at the University of Cambridge. She is author *of Chagos Islanders in Mauritius and the UK: Forced Displacement and Onward Migration* (Manchester: Manchester University Press, 2011), and holds a Research Fellowship funded by the UK Economic and Social Research Council (ESRC) to study debates about environmental knowledge in the Chagos Archipelago.

Tobias Kelly is based at the University of Edinburgh, UK. His research and teaching interests are in the broad area of political and legal anthropology. He has a particular interest in multi-sited transnational research, and has carried out fieldwork in the Middle East, the UK and at the UN. He has taught research methods at both postgraduate and undergraduate levels.

Natalie Konopinski received her Ph.D. in Social Anthropology from the University of Edinburgh, UK, and has taught anthropological research methods to undergraduate and M.Sc. level students. Her research explores security practices, anticipation, protection and the state in Israel. She is currently Visiting Scholar at the School for Conflict Analysis and Resolution at George Mason University, USA, where she is writing her monograph *Securityland: Anticipation, Suspicion and Citizenship in Tel Aviv.*

Neil Thin is a social anthropologist at the University of Edinburgh, UK, with 30 years of combined experience in research, planning, policy-making and grassroots activity in the UK, South Asia, South-East Asia, Africa, and Latin America. His research, teaching, and advisory work is always interdisciplinary, focusing on the intercultural understanding and promotion of well-being and happiness through social policies and development interventions. He is the author of *Social Progress and Sustainable Development* (Rugby: ITDG Publications, 2002) and *Social Happiness: Research into Policy and Practice* (Bristol: Policy Press, 2012) as well as many policy, research and training documents for international development organizations.

Acknowledgements

Thanks to Lesley Riddle and Katherine Ong at Routledge for their hard work and enthusiasm. A big thanks to all the students we have taught, whose research projects have helped us refine our advice and ideas for this book.

Introduction

About *Doing Anthropological Research*

Natalie Konopinski

Who this book is for

This book is for anyone who is preparing, conducting and writing an anthropology research project. It is particularly intended for advanced undergraduate and graduate students who will be carrying out short-term research and producing a dissertation over the course of a university semester or summer.

For many students the chance to put their learning into practice is the most exciting and satisfying part of an anthropology degree. A research project – whether you are delving into the archives, doing research in the library, heading into 'the field', or all three – can be a stimulating and deeply rewarding experience. Research may also be daunting and even difficult at times. Above all it offers the chance to join a particular anthropological conversation and pursue your own research interests. This book aims to help you navigate your way through the process and make the most of it.

Why are you reading this book? Perhaps you are about to begin your first research project and wonder how to fashion your ideas into an actual topic for research. Perhaps you need advice about how to engage with secondary resources or write a research proposal. You might be in the middle of your project asking how to analyze the myriad fieldnotes, documents and visual materials you have collected. Maybe you are an aspiring Malinowski with plans to carry out ethnographic fieldwork. Or, perhaps you are interested in the kinds of anthropology carried out online, among historical archives or library shelves. Whatever your research stage or questions, for practical advice about the process of doing your own anthropological research, read on.

What this book aims to do

This book is a practical guide to doing your own anthropology research project. It is not just about ethnographic fieldwork or dissertation writing alone. Instead, *Doing Anthropological Research* aims to help you manage all the elements of a research project, from formulating a research topic to submitting a final dissertation. It is a functional how-to guide to the thought processes and practical skills you need to design a relevant, interesting project, develop your own research style, and write a successful dissertation. It aims to demystify the research process and focus on the kinds of issues all projects entail, including the ethical dimensions of doing research and the important interplay between primary research and secondary data.

Doing Anthropological Research is guided by the sorts of decisions and dilemmas students confront when preparing, conducting and writing up a research project. It draws on our collective experience as teachers and supervisors of students and their research projects across many areas of social and cultural anthropology. It also stems from our own experiences carrying out research and writing under-graduate and Ph.D. dissertations, our research successes and the mistakes we made along the way. We aim to make it as accessible, pertinent and useful as possible. This book will not tell you what to do, or do all the work for you, however. What it will do is equip you with the tools you need to prepare your project, leave the lecture theatre behind and do it yourself with confidence.

As you may have already discovered, anthropological research is not about following prescriptive rules or painting by numbers. While anthropology does possess its own share of institutional and disciplinary conventions it is also very flexible and wide-ranging in its intellectual questions and concerns. This is one of the joys of doing anthropological research. Whatever project you undertake, your research will require you to make a series of choices about the kind of discipline you take anthropology to be, about the topic you will explore, the sources you will consult, and the methods you will apply, among many others. At every step the decisions you make will need to be considered, appropriate and justifiable. Is your research topic of anthropological interest? How do you intend to answer your research questions? How will you analyze your research materials? Can you synthesize and situate your own arguments within larger anthropological and theoretical concerns? This book will help you to think through the issues and make informed decisions as you go about your project.

Despite all our preparatory work and research proposals, anthropological research always includes a degree of serendipity and the unexpected. Anthro-pology is an inherently unpredictable, iterative process and research projects will often involve the odd detour, tangent and even wrong turn. The things you discover during fieldwork or research will shape the various directions you take. There is a balance to be struck between the more unruly and systematic parts of the process, between adopting an efficient, methodical research strategy and remaining open to the surprises and opportunities that may arise along the way. Doing research, and doing it well, requires an element of flexibility and the ability to embrace the more idiosyncratic *and* systematic modes of analysis and research.

Doing independent research and producing a substantial piece of academic work is no easy task. The process of conducting and writing research is often a personal as well as an intellectual challenge. You will invariably find yourself faced with situations to navigate and problems to solve. You may also be working some distance away from your existing support networks of friends and family. As the book progresses, several chapters will address these more emotional aspects of doing research and the ordinary periods of anxiety that are part of almost all research projects.

For many students, financial circumstances and career prospects form an important part of a research project. Some students need to work part-time in order to fund research and living costs. Some may use a research project to acquire particular skills and enhance particular attributes. Others wish to improve their knowledge of an issue or field related to future career plans and ambitions. Doing your own, independent research project will help you develop a range of critical learning and communication skills that can be applied to further university study and/or working life beyond.

Organization of the book

While the sequence of chapters reflects the general chronological progress of a research project, reality rarely resembles such discrete steps or tidy structure. Many of your research activities will overlap or take place concurrently. Reading and analysis do not simply follow data collection, for example, but begin with the planning of a project and continue throughout the entire research process. The use of secondary sources may precede, accompany, follow or even replace a period of primary ethnographic 'fieldwork' or research. Visual techniques may be used to generate ideas, prompt conversation with informants, or provide detailed research outputs. Writing is an almost continuous activity and takes different forms, each fulfilling a different purpose, from ideas hastily scribbled on a page, to reading notes and fieldnotes, or a final dissertation. Other themes such as language and ethics resonate and reappear across the chapters of this book just as they do in research practice. We have tried to ensure that the content of each chapter and the cross-references we include reflect these relationships and the more fluid realities of conducting anthropological research.

In order to accurately reflect the research experience, the decisions you will need to make and the dilemmas you may face, each chapter follows two fictional students and their respective anthropology projects. Fictional they may be, but the choices our students make and the challenges they must overcome are based on our extensive experience doing research, teaching, supervising, and assessing undergraduate and postgraduate research projects.

The ways in which you choose to use this book will depend upon your own working habits, research style and immediate requirements. *Doing Anthropological Research* can be read as a constant companion or referred to periodically, at particular points along the research process. The chapters are written (more or less) sequentially but may also be read as stand-alone guides to a particular issue or stage of research. When you use it, how often and to what degree is up to you and your research needs. We should also note that *Doing Anthropological Research* is designed to accompany your university courses about research and the advice of your project supervisor. *Doing Anthropological Research* is one resource – an indispensable one, we hope – among many others you should address during the planning, conducting and writing of your research project. We have included bibliographic references at the end of each chapter and recommendations for further reading and online resources can be found on the companion website.

Doing Anthropological Research is the product of a collaborative writing endeavour between a group of social anthropologists at the University of Edinburgh. The book is an extension of several long-running and successful courses we teach to prepare our students for research. While the book as a whole represents our joint efforts, the individual contributors are indicated in the following paragraphs.

Chapter 1 (Tobias Kelly) begins with the question of how to fashion an interesting and feasible topic for an anthropology research project. What is anthropology? What are your own anthropological interests? How do you turn your ideas into a topic and series of questions for research? This chapter discusses how to start generating ideas and answering large anthropological questions with a small self-contained research project.

Chapter 2 (Laura Jeffery and Natalie Konopinski) focuses on the practicalities of preparing for research. How do you turn your topic, ideas and questions into a viable plan and research proposal? This chapter guides you through the details and design of a research proposal, including language proficiency, permissions and contacts, research methods, ethical issues, budgets, and the setting of a realistic timetable for your project.

Chapter 3 (Neil Thin) tackles the importance, use and analysis of secondary research for all anthropological research projects. Why is secondary research a crucial aspect of anthropology? What is the relationship between 'primary' and 'secondary' research? How can you find and use a variety of information sources – libraries, documents, books, databases, websites and articles – for your research? This chapter discusses secondary research for preparation purposes as well as suggesting ways in which secondary sources may form a key object of ethnographic analysis. It offers advice on ways to develop an enjoyable, efficient, systematic and transparent system for accessing and evaluating primary, secondary and tertiary resources.

Chapter 4 (Joost Fontein) focuses on the relationship between anthropology and ethnographic fieldwork. What anthropological assumptions or perspectives are embedded within your own research plan? What kinds of methods and approaches will your project require? Using the work of four anthropologists, this chapter takes a more detailed look at the relationship that exists between research questions, theoretical or anthropological perspectives and fieldwork methods.

Chapter 5 (Joost Fontein) addresses different fieldwork techniques and the practical aspects of conducting ethnographic fieldwork. It offers constructive advice about where and how to live, how to prepare for research contingencies, how to begin generating information, and how to turn your fieldwork encounters into usable forms of ethnographic data.

Chapter 6 (Ian Harper) addresses the ethical dimensions of doing anthropological research. It looks beyond ethical review procedures and permissions to ask: 'what are "ethics" in the context of an anthropology research project?'

This chapter examines our relations and responsibilities to ourselves and to others throughout the research process, using a series of anthropological controversies and ethical case studies to help you think through the issues and reflect on your own research project.

Chapter 7 (Lotte Hoek) addresses the process of managing your empirical research data and developing anthropological arguments. It provides a series of organizational and analytical steps through which to begin sorting and interpreting your materials, linking theory with data and articulating your analysis.

Chapter 8 (John Harries) deals with the process of communicating your research and composing a dissertation in anthropology. It guides you through the business of planning to write and getting it done: from forming a plausible and credible argument, to practical ways in which to situate your own detailed, provisional analysis within broader theoretical and anthropological arguments. It includes tips on structuring your discussion and suggests ways in which to get started, stay sane and submit your dissertation.

Each chapter contains a series of key points to clarify discussion and help you reflect on your own project as you make your way through the research process. The web pages that accompany *Doing Anthropological Research* contain useful ancillary materials such as practical exercises, tips on writing style and presentation, as well as suggestions for further reading and online resources should you wish to read more widely or in more depth on a particular subject. It can be accessed via the Routledge website at www.routledge.com/cw/konopinski.

1   Getting started

The search for anthropological questions

Tobias Kelly

This chapter examines how to come up with a viable and interesting topic for an anthropology research project. The key issue is to focus down on a relatively small-scale, self-contained project that can also be used to address issues of wider analytical and comparative importance. This chapter discusses different approaches to the posing of distinctively anthropological problems, and explores the relationship between library- and fieldwork-based dissertations. It also stresses that a successful choice of topic will bear in mind the existing skills of the student, as well as those that they wish to develop.

Coming up with a research topic

What sort of topics make for the best anthropological research projects? There is no simple answer to this, and the best projects can be very varied indeed. However, one thing is probably universally true about all good projects: they have a specific focus. Focusing down on a specific topic or issue can be very difficult, particularly if you are interested in lots of things. However, it is worth spending considerable time thinking about what exactly it is that you want to study and why, as it will make the research and the writing up a great deal easier.

Anthropologists are historically very bad at coming up with specific questions. There once was a time when they would simply head off somewhere, find themselves a village, live there for a few years, and write about as many aspects of life as they possibly could. They did not need explicit questions, as they were studying everything. There was also a sense that you did not want to limit what you found by overly narrow research questions. The assumption was that it was therefore best to slowly absorb what was going on, without any pre-conceived ideas about what the important issues were.

However, for several reasons, such an approach is not really tenable any more, if it ever was. It is particularly ill-suited to a student research project. Limitations on time mean that you cannot simply try to collect information about everything that goes on. If you have a few months to carry out the research, you have to get very specific, and find ways of distinguishing between what is relevant and what is not. If you try to record everything you will be overwhelmed. Equally importantly, most research projects do have questions behind them, even if they are left implicit or vague, so it is therefore useful to work out what these are early on.

If you can come up with some way of narrowing down your research it will therefore be of great help. This may seem obvious, but you would be surprised by how few people do it. Precisely because it is hard people often skip it, or hope it will become clear later. However, spending time on it right at the beginning before you dive in will help you in all sorts of ways. It will make carrying out the research that much easier as you will be able to work out what sorts of information you will need. It will also stop people giving you blank looks when you give them a ten-minute rather vague explanation of what your project is about. If you can give them a two-line answer they are much more likely to agree to be interviewed or to give you access. Having a specific question will also make reading the secondary literature that much easier, as it will help you identify the key texts that have tried to answer similar questions. Finally, it will also make writing up your project that much easier, as it will give you a structure around which to write. Ideally, this means coming up with one, two or several questions. It is important to remember though that these questions may change and need tweaking as you go along and realize that they do not quite fit what you are finding out, or there are more interesting issues to explore. However, starting out with some good questions will mean that you set off on the right foot. How then do you come up with a suitable question or topic? This chapter will try to help you find ways to do so.

Key points

- Coming up with specific questions early on will help you focus at all stages of the research project.

What is anthropology about anyway?

One of the first things to think about is what exactly is anthropology about? Doing so will help you reflect about what the actual aim of your research project is and how you can go about formulating your questions, or identifying the issues you want to examine. The first thing to do is not to get hung up over the differences between cultural and social anthropology. For all practical purposes, they are pretty much the same thing. The next thing to do is to let go of the sense that there is some great big secret to anthropology. It is a very common student experience to feel one does not understand what anthropology is all about, and to hope that at some point it will all simply fall into place. I am afraid this will probably not happen. One of the great attractions of anthropology for many people is its very disparateness, and this can be liberating. The third thing to do is remember that the issue of 'what anthropology is about' is different from the analytical or theoretical frameworks you use. You do not need to decide if you are structuralist, or a Marxist, or a whatever right now. You need to think about what your questions are about before you decide how you are going to answer them. Theoretical perspectives will become important later on and we will deal with them in Chapters 4 and 7. The final and perhaps most important thing to do is try to think about what it was that drew you to anthropology in the first place. What was it that made you pick up an anthropology book or sign up for an anthropology course? What were the types of questions that you hoped you would find the answers to? Try to uncover some of that initial enthusiasm that may have got lost as you prepare for exams or write essays. A research project can be an immense amount of fun, and probably the most interesting thing you will do during your degree, so treat it as something to enjoy rather than dread.

There are dozens of different ways of understanding the anthropological project. You do not have to choose between them, and indeed, many practicing anthropologists will hold to several different definitions at the same time. Different departments might emphasize some over others, but it would be very rare for a department to stick to any one definition.

For some people anthropology is simply the 'attempt to understand the internal logic of another society'. This is an approach that assumes that societies can be understood as wholes, as distinct units. People attracted to this approach would therefore try to locate a particular society and then study how it fits together. Much classic anthropology can be seen as taking this direction. Evans-Pritchard, for example, went to what is now Southern Sudan in the 1930s and produced books that claimed to show the Nuer religious system, Nuer economics, Nuer kinship and Nuer politics (see, for example, Evans-Pritchard 1987). Such an approach is attractive to some people because it stresses that you should not dismiss other ways of doing things simply because they are different, but instead you should try to understand them on their own terms. Critics would argue, though, that this approach is in danger of treating societies as if they are static and organic objects. The assumption is that you can compare, for example, 'Scottish society', with 'Nuer society' or 'Malay society'. Anyone who has ever been to Scotland, or Southern Sudan or Malaysia will be able to tell you that these are very diverse places, and that it is very difficult to see any kind of overriding or consistent logic at play in the way in which people go about things.

Another way of thinking about anthropology is as the 'comparative study of societies and cultures'. Although very few projects are directly comparative, they more often than not involve an implicit comparison. Malinowski, for example, was interested in the patterns of gift giving among the Trobriand Islanders of what is now Papua New Guinea, not simply because he thought they were interesting in and of themselves (see, for example, Malinowski 1978). More importantly, the system of economic exchange and political alliance based on the continual transfer of seashells offered a direct counterpoint to the economic and political systems of Europe and North America. Making comparisons between the ways in which people go about things in different places, can help us understand what is specific to a particular place, and what is part of a more general phenomenon. In practice such comparisons are seldom made explicit, and this is perhaps one of the most common failings of much anthropology. However, there are good practical reasons for this. It can be hard enough to carry out a project in one place, let alone two. Especially in the context of a student research project, choosing two places can make the project simply unwieldy.

Another approach that is linked to the one in the preceding paragraph sees anthropology as the 'attempt to make the peculiar look mundane and the mundane look peculiar'. This approach is often comparative, but not necessarily so. More importantly, it is an attempt to challenge what are often seen as taken for granted or universal assumptions about the way we live our lives. On the one hand, this means looking at practices that at first glance look to be a bit wacky and exotic, and then showing how, in their own terms, they make perfect sense. In many ways this is a very traditional anthropological approach, and can be seen in Malinowski's attempts to understand Trobriand economics, or Evans-Pritchard's attempts to examine Nuer religion, for example. On the other hand, this also means trying to show that things that we often assume are self-evident or banal, are actually weird, wonderful and peculiar. Such an approach is often associated with what is sometimes called 'anthropology at home', that is, research on North America and Europe. Caitlin Zaloom (2004), for example, has studied the culture of stock market traders in New York and London, and shown how it is every bit as strange as Trobriand or Nuer economic systems. Perhaps an even better example is Margaret Lock's comparative study of organ transplants in the US and Japan, *Twice Dead* (2001). In this book Lock takes something seemingly as self-evident as death, and shows how attitudes to what counts as death, and when it takes place, are very different in the US and Japan.

Rather than the type of questions it asks, another approach to anthropology sees it as defined by its methods: primary ethnographic fieldwork. From this perspective what marks out anthropology is its commitment to the ethnographic method. It is because anthropologists go out there and live among the people they are studying for long periods of time that they can produce fine-grained, textured and qualitative accounts of what actually happens on the ground. Once again, this is not a new approach to anthropology, and can be seen as stretching back to the early twentieth century. However, the things that we study have changed. Whereas anthropologists may well have once tried to study what they saw as 'traditional' small-scale societies, often seen as being located in villages, in the twenty-first century they can equally be found in factories, human rights organizations, hospitals and prisons, among other places. However, it should be noted that anthropology is now far from being the only discipline that carries out ethnographic fieldwork. There are strong ethnographic traditions in sociology and geography, as well as other disciplines. Furthermore, not all anthropology or ethnography is necessarily based on long-term fieldwork. 'Ethnography' also includes secondary research methods and many works of anthropology are theoretical, or based on secondary sources (see Chapter 3 for more on this topic). Those of you who are thinking about library-based dissertations should therefore not necessarily think of them as a second-best option. There is a long tradition of very fine and influential anthropology based on secondary sources.

A further way of looking at anthropology is simply as 'philosophy with the people left in'. Whereas philosophers might try to answer questions about the nature of knowledge, or being, for example, in the abstract, anthropologists try to answer such questions with reference to what people actually do and say. Anthropologists are interested in the same questions as philosophers, but try to answer them in a different, largely ethnographic, way. If a philosopher tries to answer questions such as 'how do we know that other people exist?' through deductive reason or logic, an anthropologist would try to understand how people on the ground themselves grapple with this problem and what types of answers they come up with. More specifically, it is possible to understand anthropology as a form of humanistic philosophy. This is to say that anthropology seeks to answer the specific philosophical question, 'what is it that makes us human?' As a fundamentally comparative discipline anthropology is well placed to examine what it is that all human beings have in common.

Finally, anthropology can be understood as a political project, in that its purpose can be seen as the attempt to 'make the world safe for human differences'. Given that anthropologists often explore the meanings and implications of human difference, anthropology can be seen as part of a progressive project to make human difference more acceptable. Early twentieth-century anthropologists were often, but not always, part of wider anti-colonial and anti-racist projects, and they saw their task as about challenging prejudice. Franz Boas, often seen as one of the founding figures of American anthropology, was, for example, a prominent critic of racist ideologies. It might be argued though that the anthropological emphasis on difference has often blinded anthropologists to injustices. The claim of cultural difference can be used to justify practices, such as what is often called 'female genital mutilation'. More broadly, the fact that anthropologists spend a great deal of time with the people they work with, and develop long-lasting relationships with them, means that many anthropologists argue they have a moral and political responsibility to campaign on their behalf (Scheper-Hughes 1995). In response it might be claimed that although such an approach is well meaning, it is questionable whether anthropologists are the best and most appropriate people to bring about political change. To think that we are is just self-important. The debate here is long and contentious, and there is not the space here to go into it in detail. The point is simply to raise the argument that anthropology, for some people, cannot simply be an academic project, but must also be inherently political.

All these perspectives have their own adherents, as well as critics, and there are many more that have not been mentioned. You may well have your own ideas. What is important is that before you embark on your project you think about what the larger discipline is about and therefore the types of issues you might want to address. If you think anthropology is about making the peculiar mundane or the mundane peculiar, you will try to find sites of peculiarity or apparent mundaneness and think of ways of turning them on their head. If you think anthropology is 'philosophy with the people left in' you will seek to answer philosophical questions. If you think anthropology is a fundamentally political project, you will seek to address fundamentally political issues. If you think anthropology is ultimately about ethnographic fieldwork, you will focus on the insights that fieldwork can give us, and so on.

Key points

- Decide what sort of project or discipline you think anthropology is.

The rest of this chapter and the rest of the book will use two concrete examples of students developing their own projects in order to better illustrate how the process might work.

First, let us start with **Janet**. Janet is an undergraduate student preparing for a long essay or dissertation in her final year. Since she started her degree she has become increasingly interested in philosophy, and the types of anthropology she finds most interesting are those that address big philosophical questions about the nature of life and death. However, she also finds philosophy too abstract, and what she likes most about anthropology is the way in which it is always linked to what real people do, think and say. Janet therefore decided that she wanted to undertake a project that would ask big philosophical questions but through ethnographic examples.

Our second example is **John**. John was initially attracted to anthropology because he thought it would help him to understand different cultures and societies. However, as he set about preparing for his long essay or dissertation in his final year he realized that what interested him most was not the exotic, but the seemingly familiar. He enjoyed reading those books that made him question things about his own life that he had previously taken for granted. He therefore decided that he wanted to do a project that would hopefully do the same.

Think practical

The next step is to think practical. This means thinking about what skills you will need to carry out a piece of research and which skills you have. If you will need to speak a foreign language and you currently do not speak any, you need to be realistic about the type of research you can do. Fieldwork in rural China is probably out. If your only language is English, then stick to topics where you only need a command of English. You will be amazed by how many people head to the Amazon jungle, and then realize that without a command of at least two new languages, they are not going to get very far. Language is such an important issue for any project that we will look at it again in Chapters 2 and 5.

Research in far-flung and exotic places can also be very expensive. It is not just flights, but accommodation, visas and insurance that you need to think about as well. There is very little funding for this type of research. If you are going to need to work, it makes sense to choose a topic that you can do whilst working at the same time. This might mean working closer to home, finding a job where you want to carry out the research, or carrying out a primarily secondary or library-based research project.

Having said all this, undertaking anthropological research can also offer the opportunity to stretch yourself and develop new skills that go beyond the research project itself. It can be used as an opportunity to improve language skills, for example. Probably more importantly, many people use their long piece of undergraduate research as a way of making them more employable. If you want to work in a particular field afterwards, think of a topic or issue that is related to that field. Not only might it help you make contacts, but it can also provide you with new skills and prove to any future employer that you have a genuine interest in the area. If you want to go into theatre management, think about projects around the theatre. If you want to work in international development, think about projects linked to international development issues. If you want to become a teacher, think about projects that are linked to education.

Finally, and perhaps most importantly, you need to make sure that you will be happy and comfortable throughout the project. It is one thing to stretch yourself and put yourself in new situations. However, there is no need to make yourself miserable. In part, this means thinking about what actually interests you. You are going to be spending large amounts of time on this project, involving many hours alone reading in libraries and writing at your desk. It is therefore important that you choose a topic that will keep you enthusiastic all the way through. Furthermore, you also need to make sure that you are personally happy. If you have people who you rely on and who rely on you, there is no need to separate yourself from them.

Key points

- Think about what skills you already have and which you can use to your advantage in the research project.
- Think about skills you want to develop for future plans and the ways this project might help you develop them.
- Remember that there is no point in sacrificing your well-being for a project.

Janet had initially thought she wanted to go to India, but then realized that as she did not speak any of the relevant languages, this would probably not be very sensible. She did, however, speak good Spanish, after studying it at school and spending a year living in Spain as a child. She therefore decided it would make sense to carry out her fieldwork in a Spanish-speaking country. She had been working all year and managed to save some money so she thought she could afford to travel abroad if she wanted to. Janet was not at all sure what she wanted to do when she graduated, and furthermore, one of the reasons she liked anthropology was that it gave her space to explore issues without attaching an instrumental value to them. She therefore decided that she would use her research to help improve her Spanish, but was not going to design it with some future job in mind.

John was much more concerned than Janet about life after university. He had strong interests in the broad area of social policy and was convinced that anthropological insights could be very useful in this field. He only spoke English, so this also limited where he might want to go. John decided to stay in the UK and carry out some research that might make him more employable to social policy–type organizations, through developing both skills and contacts in the sector.

Home or away, fieldwork or library-based?

Students often feel that they have to study some far away or exotic place. Indeed this may be in part what first attracted them to study anthropology in the first place. However, you can do just as interesting a project close to 'home'. If you think, for example, that anthropology is about making the mundane peculiar or the peculiar mundane, there are plenty of both peculiar and mundane things to study that do not require travelling to the ends of the earth. The trick is to be imaginative in where you look for them. Football matches, stag weekends, internet dating, science fiction conventions, organic food markets, self-help groups, or for that matter universities, all offer as much potential as an initiation ritual in the Kenyan desert. Indeed, for many people, the distinction between anthropology 'at home' and anthropology 'out there' is no longer valid, if it ever was. On one level, you are likely to find the same institutions, practices and commodities in Peru, as in Papua New Guinea or Belgium. On another level, it is not clear to many people where 'home' exactly is. Students, lecturers and members of the general public move around all the time for work, study or family reasons.

Wherever you end up doing your research it is important that you find ways of preventing yourself from taking what you see or hear for granted. This does not mean thinking that everyone is lying to you. Rather, it means that you need to remember that things can always be otherwise. There is nothing inevitable about the way things are. This is partly why many anthropologists have gone to new places which they know little about. It is easier to keep that sense of bemusement or surprise when things are not so familiar. However, it is still possible, although harder, to do so in contexts within which you are already deeply embedded. You need to find ways to constantly trip yourself up, or to step back and ask questions about what you are finding out. Carrying out research in an area about which you already know a great deal comes with the added benefit that you can hit the ground running. This is all just to say that there are advantages and disadvantages in carrying out research in contexts with which you are familiar or unfamiliar, and it is not that one is better than the other. You need to think about what sort of context suits your personal situation and interests.

Many anthropology students feel that they should undertake primary fieldwork. Long-term ethnographic immersion has been a rite of passage for professional anthropologists for a long time. Fieldwork can also be an immense amount of fun and profoundly interesting in its own right. However, it may be that some projects are much better thought of as secondary or library-based. Once again, such projects should in no way be thought as second best in comparison to fieldwork-based research, just different. If you want to write about suicide bombers, for example, participant observation is obviously out of the question. Topics that might produce ethical problems for the researcher or the people they are researching are probably best conducted in a library, as are issues around which you might not get access to the key people. Library-based research may include an analysis of what other people have written on a topic. It can also include an examination of primary texts, such as archival material, newspapers and policy documents. In truth, the contrast between library and fieldwork topics is not hard and fast. Even if you do decide to go off to the Amazon jungle you will still need to do background reading. Before deciding on a primarily library-based project, though, it is very important that you make sure that there are enough secondary resources for you to carry out the project. If no one has written about male prostitutes in rural Russia, you should probably think of doing something else. There are also key practical advantages of doing a library-based piece of research. Not only can you stay close to 'home', but, on the whole, your sources are not going to be too busy to talk to you.

Key points

- There is no need to go somewhere that seems superficially exotic to carry out research.
- Wherever you carry out your research you will need to find ways to prevent yourself from taking things for granted.
- Some types of research topic may be better suited to secondary or library research.

Janet did not want to go to Spain and had always wanted to try Latin America. She had friends who lived in Mexico so settled on there.

John strongly believed that you should be able to carry out research in the UK as much as some far-flung place, and so settled on fieldwork in his home town.

Thinking both big and small

It is now time to start focusing down. The trick with coming up with a good topic or question is to find a nice discrete issue or fieldwork site through which you can address larger questions. Given the amount of time and resources that you will probably have available, it is very important that you do not bite off more than you can chew. Too large a project, where the information you can collect and the questions you can ask about it keep on going for ever and ever, is simply going to be impractical. It will also result in a final written document that will be unfocused and cover too many issues superficially. It is therefore important that you find a topic that you know how to cut off at the edges. At the same time, you do not want a topic that is too small and obscure. Your choice of topic will have to enable you to look at issues that are of broader social scientific importance. Studying home-brewed beer enthusiasts, for example, simply for the sake of studying home-brewed beer enthusiasts will probably not produce a very interesting research project. You have got to think of why home-brew enthusiasts might be relevant to anthropology and of interest to other people.

It is important therefore that you find a way of linking 'small places' with 'large issues' (Eriksen 2001). There are two ways of going about this. The first is to think about what broader issues interest you, and then try to think of ways in which you can ground these issues. If you are interested in migration, or the social implications of fertility, or the nature of political activism, you need to think about the sorts of places where you could do research on these issues. The greatest projects at the abstract level can fall apart if you cannot think of any- where that you can do the research. The other way is to think about what sort of places you might like to do research on, and then think about what broader issues you might be able to explore through these sites. In the end it does not matter which way you start, as long as you end up in the same place. The same goes for library research. Even if you are primarily using documentary resour- ces, you will still need to narrow it down into a bite-sized chunk.

It might help to give a few concrete examples. An organic farmers' market would be a very good place to examine an issue such as the relationship between nature and culture. A stable would be a wonderful place to examine issues around human–animal relations. If you are interested in issues around parenting and kinship, an antenatal class would be a good place to start. If your burning passion is factory work, fieldwork in a factory would allow you to explore issues to do with creativity and exchange. If you have always wanted to spend time in a Hindu temple, fieldwork in such a place would enable you to explore issues around ritual and religious practice.

Another way of going about this is to look at some of your favourite eth- nographies and think about how they try to relate discrete ethnographic research to issues of larger import. Annelise Riles (1999), for example, uses her fieldwork carried out in a Fijian human rights organization that was preparing for a UN conference, as a way of examining issues such as the nature of human rights in a 'globalizing' world. She used the ethnography of the everyday practices of the NGO workers to ask questions about what it might actually mean to say that human rights are globalized. Loïc Wacquant (2007) used his work in a Chicago boxing gym to examine issues to do with masculinity and the relationship between sport and violence. Lorraine Danforth used a comparative analysis of fire-walking in Greece and the US to examine issues to do with suffering and religious healing (1989).

Key points

- Try to think of a relatively small research site that enables you to address broader questions.
- Do not bite off more than you can chew.

What does a field site look like?

Do not assume that you need a single fieldwork site. The days of everyone having to limit their fieldwork to one small village are long gone, if they were ever here at all. There are various ways of thinking about your research site. One way, probably the most traditional, is as a discrete location. This means doing fieldwork in one particular place. This does not necessarily mean a village. It can be a neighbourhood of a town or city. Equally, it could be an institution, such as a school, NGO, government bureaucracy, or even a library. The upside of this approach is that it is focused and you know where you have to go every morning. The downside is that people may be too busy to talk to you. If you do research in a work environment, it may be hard to get people to stop work to spend time with you. If you work in a residential area, people may be off at work all day, and when they get home the last thing they might want to do is spend time with an anthropologist. Perhaps most importantly, if you stick to one place there may simply be nothing interesting going on, and you will be left with little to write about.

Another way of thinking about the field site is that it focuses on a process or an issue. This means following the issue wherever it takes you. The downside of this is that it can get out of hand very quickly and you can lose focus. The upside is that you can get different perspectives on the same topic and collect all sorts of different information, adding depth and colour to your research. A good example of this approach is Alexander Edmonds' (2011) book on beauty and plastic surgery in Brazil. Edmonds was interested in why plastic surgery was so popular in Brazil. His initial interest was sparked by a carnival float dedicated to a plastic surgeon. Rather than focus on a plastic surgeon's clinic, however, he spent time with socialites, watched TV soap operas, hung out in the waiting rooms of public hospitals that offered plastic surgery, and interviewed maids and their elite mistresses, divorced housewives, black celebrities, and favela residents aspiring to be fashion models. The end result is a not based on a specific location, but is held together by looking for those places where a desire for plastic surgery was produced and reproduced.

When thinking about what your fieldwork site might look like, it is also important that you think very practically. The first thing to think about is access. Are people going to let you carry out work in a hospital or an office, or anywhere else for that matter? We may be desperate to do fieldwork in a mosque, or a courtroom, or a scientific laboratory, but why should the people who live or work there necessarily agree to spend time with you? They probably live busy lives already and researchers can be very annoying. Even if they do agree to let you in, negotiating access can take a long time, something you might not have. This is not to say that you should not seek permission, but simply that you should be aware that it can be difficult. Some of the greatest projects collapse because researchers are not allowed in. Access is an issue throughout research, and will be covered again in Chapters 2 and 5.

Key points

- A field site can be a discrete location, such as an office or village, or a process, such as the beauty industry.
- Think about whether you will be able to gain practical access.

Janet was interested in large-scale philosophical questions about life and death. Life seemed to be far too big for her to deal with so she settled on death. At least death was a specific moment, she thought, whereas life stretched on for years. Her family and lecturers were initially worried that this would be too morbid, and tried to persuade her otherwise, but she was convinced it was a good topic. The next step was to think of a place where she could carry out the research. One example she thought of was an old people's home, as people die there all the time. However, she decided that this could be intrusive, as well as upsetting, especially for herself. Being a fan of the TV series *Six Feet Under* she then settled on an undertakers. She decided that she would try to seek work as an assistant for a Mexican funeral director. That way she would not have to deal with grieving relatives. It would give her a great place to start examining how Mexicans dealt with and prepared for death. However, she was slightly worried about whether she would be able to persuade a Mexican funeral director to allow her to work with them behind the scenes.

John had much more difficulty settling on a topic. Part of the problem was that he was interested in lots of different things. In the end he settled on an issue that would allow him to bring together many of these disparate interests. He had become interested in the notion of luck, how some people explain fortune and misfortune, and what implications this has for the ways they live their lives. One way to narrow this down seemed to be by focusing on the issue of gambling. Gambling was attractive to him because it had social policy implications in terms of gambling addiction. He still had to decide what type of gambling he wanted to focus on, and decided to look at greyhound-racing. He had initially thought about horseracing, but realized that the nearest race track was miles from his house. There was, however, a greyhound track a short bus-ride away. He would therefore have to try to negotiate access there. John also realized that there were plenty of other places where he could carry out research on the issue. These included grey-hound trainers' kennels and bookmakers' shops, as well as organizations concerned with gambling addiction.

From first-order to second-order questions

Once you have decided what you think anthropology is about, worked out your practical limitations, addressed the ways in which research might be able to help you develop further skills, thought of some big themes and linked them to research sites, it is time to start trying to generate your questions. In truth you are already most of the way there. It might simply mean putting a question mark at the end of a sentence. Often, though, it will be more difficult than that.

Start off with a broad, general question linked to your field site and then narrow it down. It is very important to narrow it down because otherwise you will not know how to organize your fieldwork or library research. If you simply ask 'what is the meaning of life?' type questions you cannot even begin to think of the kinds of information you might need to answer such a question. Imagine the looks that people will give you as well. More narrow and specific questions that speak to larger issues will help you focus down the research itself.

One way to start is with the thing that first attracted you to the issue, the incident that caught your eye. You can then pose this as a question: 'why does such and such a thing happen?' If you read a lot of anthropological articles you will notice that many of them start with a vignette or an apparent conundrum, and then ask 'how do we understand this apparently baffling or strange thing?' Alexander Edmonds' work on plastic surgery starts with the apparently simple question of why people should create a carnival float dedicated to a plastic surgeon. He then uses this very simple question to ask broader questions such as 'why do poor people spend money on plastic surgery?' In a very different example Michael Gilsenan (1996) asks why men in 1970s rural Lebanon spend so much time sitting around telling often wild and wonderful stories about each other. He uses this simple question in order to then explore bigger questions such as 'what role does language have in the reproduction of power inequalities?'

Another way of going about formulating specific questions is to start at the other end, and try to turn your big issue or question into a context-specific question. If you are interested, for example, in the nature of pain and healing, and have settled on a community of new age firewalkers as your research site, you need to bring your questions down to a level where they are directly applicable to that situation. This means asking, for example, 'why do people think walking on burning coals will heal them?' If you are interested in British masculinity, and have settled on stag weekends in coastal resort towns, this might mean, for example, asking, 'why do British men like to dress up in women's clothes just before they get married?' If you are interested in issues of birth and reproduction, and have settled on an antenatal group, you might ask, for example, 'what do people mean when they talk about a natural birth, and why do they see this as preferable?'

Box 1.1

Concept maps, mind maps and napkin sketches

You may also find it useful to engage in some visual thinking as a way of quickly gaining a confident sense of what your key research questions are and how they can be communicated. All these approaches, particularly if done collaboratively, offer ways of usefully visualizing your research issue/s, coming up with ideas, and making connections between them. A concept map is a top-down diagram that shows relationships among concepts. Mind maps are radial, hierarchical diagrams that allow you to chart relations and associations between ideas, concepts and information. Napkin sketching is a way to identify problems and solutions with very simple pictures. Either way, forcing yourself to get things down on paper can be a very useful way of clarifying, sorting and prioritizing your ideas. Some people think visually, others in narrative form. Find the best way for yourself.

Some useful references:

Tony Buzan's mind-mapping website (this also has some good, free introductory videos and tools), www.thinkbuzan.com.

Dan Roam's 'Napkin Academy' website, www.danroam.com.

Eppler, M. J. 2006. 'A Comparison between Concept Maps, Mind Maps, Conceptual Diagrams, and Visual Metaphors as Complementary Tools for Knowledge Construction and Sharing', *Information Visualization*, 5(3): 202–10.

Key points

- Link larger questions to second-order questions that refer directly to your field site.

Janet was interested in why people mark death with specific rituals. However, she had to find a way to make such a broad question relevant to the context of a Mexican funeral parlour. She therefore decided to ask two related questions. The first was: 'what motivated people to become funeral directors?' This was a good question, she thought, as it was one she could collect direct answers to by simply asking people who worked as undertakers. The second was: 'what notions of aesthetic beauty are deployed when preparing a body for burial?' This question would be more difficult to answer, but by working on the preparation of bodies and asking why people did things in specific ways she hoped she would begin to understand what was going on.

John was interested in the larger question of how people use luck to explain fortune and misfortune and the ways that they try to control this. This was too large and vague, so he had to narrow it down to the context of greyhound-racing. He therefore focused down on a very specific question. This was: 'how do people decide what dogs they are going to place their money on?' This was a very concrete question and was something he could actually ask people during fieldwork.

References

Danforth, Loring. 1989. *Firewalking and Religious Healing: The Anastenaria of Greece and the American Firewalking Movement*. Princeton: Princeton University Press.

Edmonds, Alexander. 2011. *Pretty Modern: Beauty, Sex, and Plastic Surgery in Brazil*. Durham, NC: Duke University Press.

Evans-Pritchard, E. E. 1987 (1940). *The Nuer: A Description of the Modes of Livelihood and Political Institutions of a Nilotic People*. New York and Oxford: Oxford University Press.

Gilsenan, Michael. 1996. *Lords of the Lebanese Marches: Violence and Narrative in an Arab Society*. Oxford: I.B.Taurus.

Eriksen, Thomas H. 2001. *Small Places, Large Issues: An Introduction to Social and Cultural Anthropology*. London: Pluto.

Lock, Margaret. 2001. *Twice Dead: Organ Transplants and the Reinvention of Death*. Berkeley: University of California Press.

Malinowski, Branislaw. 1978 (1922). *Argonauts of the Western Pacific: An Account of Native Enterprise and Adventure in the Archipelagoes of Melanesian New Guinea*. London: Routledge.

Riles, Annelise. 1999. *The Network Inside Out*. Ann Arbour: Michigan University Press.

Scheper-Hughes, Nancy. 1995. 'The Primacy of the Ethical: Propositions for a Militant Anthropology', *Current Anthropology*, 36(3): 409–40.

Wacquant, Loïc. 2007 (2004). *Body and Soul: Notebooks of an Apprentice Boxer*. New York and Oxford: Oxford University Press.

Zaloom, Caitlin. 2004. *Out of the Pits: Traders and Technology from Chicago to London*. Chicago: Chicago University Press.

2 Planning your research project

Laura Jeffery and Natalie Konopinski

You have come up with your research topic, chosen your research site, and developed your research questions. What next? Now you need to plan your research more concretely. This chapter will guide you through the key considerations in preparing for research and writing a research proposal: literature review, research methods, ethical issues, language proficiency, permission and contacts, budget and timetable.

Writing your research proposal

Once you have focused your ideas and developed an interesting project you are ready to think through the practicalities of research and write your research proposal. You may need to prepare different versions of your research proposal for different audiences. First, you may need to submit a proposal to your university's anthropology department in order to get the academic go-ahead for your project. Second, you may be required to submit your proposal to your university's ethics committee or institutional review board to receive the practical and ethical permissions to conduct your research. Third, you might want to submit a proposal to funding bodies (although this tends to be extremely limited, especially for undergraduate students) to give you the financial wherewithal to bring your project to life.

A research proposal is a presentation of ideas, a plan of action and a rationale for research. A proposal explains the significance of your project, describes its broader relevance, shows how it builds on and is situated within previous research, and outlines the work you intend to do. This means providing your audience with a comprehensive plan for research, describing how your project will make a meaningful contribution to the discipline. In what ways is your proposal relevant? How does it expand existing scholarship? Can you describe and justify your chosen research topic, questions, field site/s and methods? Have you devised a feasible timetable for your project? Have you identified any ethical issues or practical pitfalls (and how will you avoid or resolve them)? Your research proposal is also evidence of your potential ability and enthusiasm. It is a formal piece of academic writing but should nevertheless convey something of your own anthropological imagination and interest.

So, if you have not done so already, now is the time to focus your research topic, refine your research questions and plan your project out on paper. While the writing of a research proposal can be a daunting prospect, the process of designing research and articulating your plans is a crucial one, not only for acquiring academic permission to proceed, but also for the smooth running and success of your project. You are not obliged to follow this plan to the letter once your research is under way. While proposals, plans and preparations are necessary, your questions and research methods will also develop as you do research. Deviations and alterations are a normal part of the process and you should prepare for these too (for more on this see Chapter 5). Your proposal is a flexible blueprint for research, bound to alter a bit as circumstances change and situations arise. One cannot begin, however, without a realistic and practical plan.

The specific format, length and assessment criteria will vary, so you should follow your own anthropology department's guidelines, but your research proposal is likely to be expected to contain the following key elements:

- a clear outline of your proposed research topic and research questions;
- a literature review, situating your project in terms of the relevant theoretical concepts and ethnographic context;
- a description and justification of your proposed research site – the country, region, town, village, community, library, or archive – in as much detail as possible;
- an account of your proposed research methods, including how using these methods in this research site will enable you to address your research questions and the theoretical issues raised in the preceding points;
- a thorough, critical consideration of the foreseeable ethical issues raised by your research and your approach to dealing with them;
- an account of the necessary practical arrangements – including language proficiency, visa and travel insurance, permissions and contacts, and travel plans – demonstrating the viability of your project;
- a budget showing estimated costs and any anticipated source/s of funding; and
- a timetable taking you from research proposal via research to communication and writing up.

The rest of this chapter will take you through some of these elements, focusing on the practical issues you will need to consider as you prepare your project.

Key points

- Focus on what is important and exciting about your proposed project, while being clear about how it contributes to the existing literature and how it is feasible within the various constraints that confront you.

Literature review

Research is not conducted in isolation, but forms part of ongoing discussion and scholarly debate. As you plan your research you will be embarking on a long relationship with academic literature and other sources that will continue throughout the life of your project. Your own research project will be informed by the work of past anthropologists and influenced by contemporary concerns, and will in turn connect to research that others will conduct in the future.

In general, a literature review is a survey of scholarly articles, books and other sources relevant to a particular area of research. It provides a description, summary and critical evaluation of the current state of scholarship. A good literature review will go beyond simple descriptions to link the proposed project with broader questions, debates and gaps in anthropological knowledge (Imel 2011), thus setting out current understandings of your topic and showing how your own project will add to this body of work.

The purpose of the literature review is to:

- place existing work in the context of its contribution to the understanding of the subject under review;
- describe the relationship of each work to the others under consideration;
- identify new ways to interpret and shed light on any gaps in previous research;
- situate and show the relevance of your own project within the broader anthropological, ethnographic, regional and philosophical literature; and
- identify areas of prior scholarship to prevent duplication of effort.

In the previous chapter we suggested that a preoccupation with analytical or theoretical frameworks is not necessary for the initial generation of ideas. When it comes to planning your project and writing a proposal, however, you will be expected to describe how your research is embedded within relevant thematic and ethnographic contexts. This means reviewing the concepts and theoretical arguments in the comparative literature related to your topic and situating your own project in terms of these. In other words, as you review the literature you begin to frame your research project and your research questions within its key concepts and themes. You may also find that your reading and review helps to refine your research questions and the broader issue/s you intend to explore. For instance, in preparing her research proposal, Janet could read up on anthropological approaches to rites of passage, death, aesthetics and the body, and Catholicism in Latin America. Meanwhile, John could engage with the literature on human–animal relations, gambling and addictions, and class politics in urban Britain. In Chapter 4 we discuss the implications of theoretical perspectives and anthropological approaches for how we do fieldwork.

Your literature review should combine *summary* and *synthesis*. A summary is a concise recap of the important information, whereas a synthesis is a reshuffling or a reorganization of that information. A quality literature review is a piece of discursive prose, not an annotated bibliography or list summarizing one item after another. Synthesize your chosen sources and organize your review into sections that provide your own insights, present themes, or identify trends. The point is not to try to list all the material published, but to synthesize and evaluate it according to the guiding concept of your research issue. The aim is to demonstrate a command of the relevant literature and make a compelling case for your research project. Good examples of literature reviews can be found in *Annual Review of Anthropology*, although your own review need not make so many original arguments and should focus more on the summary and the synthesis.

Systematic secondary research and advice for searching and surveying the literature and other sources are the subjects of Chapter 3, so flick forward for more information on how to get started. Literature research and review is a recurring feature of any anthropology project and is therefore a recurring theme within this book. You can find further discussion about literature review and analysis in Chapter 7, and on writing a dissertation in Chapter 8.

Key points

- Your literature review should show that you have identified and engaged with the theoretical and ethnographic literature relevant to your own research topic.
- Your literature review should identify the significant gaps in previous studies that your proposed research will address.

Ethnographic research methods

'Ethnography' refers to the whole process of conducting research and producing texts about culture. In practice it is often used to refer to primary fieldwork only, but this is a misleading restriction as secondary research is an extremely important source of ethnographic knowledge and inspiration throughout one's anthropological career. Whether primary or secondary, ethnographic research methods are distinctive in the degree to which they focus on interpreting qualitative information about social and cultural processes. When it comes to your own research project you will need to decide which research methods will enable you to best explore your research questions and produce meaningful results.

How are you actually going to carry out your anthropology project? What research methods will you use? And can you make any decisions about methods before you set off for fieldwork or the archives? This section of your proposal should present a clear plan for how you intend to answer your research questions and achieve your research goals. Be specific about why a particular method will be useful, how you will use it and the kind of data it will enable you to collect. Historically, anthropologists have not been renowned for the clarity with which they have explained ethnographic methods to others (to put it mildly). Fortunately, things are changing, and you are now unlikely to be packed off to the field with little more guidance than your supervisor's suggestion that you should try participant observation. Different methods can be used to address different types of research questions, and the methods that will suit an under-graduate research project entailing three months in the field or in the library are likely to differ from those that might be chosen for postgraduate fieldwork lasting a year or more. We are not going to repeat the extensive and detailed literature on research methods here. Our discussion focuses on practical planning issues and points you to specialist methods texts along the way.

Before you embark upon your research project, you should have plenty of opportunity to consider research methods:

- Browse the relevant chapters of some general ethnographic methods texts, such as those by Agar (1996); Atkinson et al. (2001); Becker (1998); Bernard (1998); Blommaert (2010); Denscombe (2010). You can find further lists of useful methods texts on the companion website.
- Critically engage with ethnographic writings in which the anthropologist discusses the methods deployed in a particular research project, such as Ferguson (1990); Messick (1993); Miller (1994); Wacquant (2002); Wilson (2001).
- Read the methods sections of some of the dissertations written by former students in your anthropology department, and think about what you might have done differently.
- Debate the advantages and disadvantages of various ethnographic methods with your peers and your supervisor.
- Consider trialing some of the suggested methods in a mini project before setting off for your primary fieldwork or secondary research in the library or other archives.

Primary fieldwork methods

The primary ethnographic or fieldwork methods you are likely to be most familiar with from your anthropology studies so far are participant observation, informal conversations, one-to-one semi-structured interviews and visual methods.

- Participant observation is the bedrock of anthropology, and entails a creative combination of participation and observation, but benefits from long-term immersion in a field site so that an increasing proportion of activities start to make sense and so that variations on a theme can be drawn into comparison with one another (see, for example, DeWalt and DeWalt 2010; Okely 2011; Watson 1999).
- Informal conversations are an invaluable way to find out what's important to the people you work with and to glean explanations of what's going on.
- Semi-structured interviews that are organized in advance may be the most effective way of getting to talk to your research participants, particularly busy elites and office-bearers – such as judges, politicians, diplomats, or civil servants – although individuals in these positions may be more likely to respond in their official capacity than provide their personal thoughts and feelings. For more about interview techniques see, for example, Atkinson and Hammersley (2007); Bernard (1998); Ritchie and Lewis (2003).

- Visual methods entail the generation and collection of visual data via the recording of social events using drawing, photography, film and digital hypermedia. Audio-visual records can be an invaluable source of non-verbal information about your ethnographic setting. Later, you may be able to use your audio-visual material in your project dissemination. Of course, your use of visual research methods will depend upon your own technical abilities, your research contexts and participants. As with all ethnographic fieldwork methods, the appropriate visual techniques, images and technologies may be most easily determined once in the field (see especially Barbash and Taylor 1997; Pink 2007, 2012; Rose 2011).

Primary fieldwork methods are notoriously time-consuming, and in a short project you may want to consider supplementing these ethnographic methods with other social science research methods – such as focus groups, questionnaires and surveys, elicitation or participatory techniques – that might help you to get background and other important information more quickly.

- Focus groups are less commonly used by anthropologists than by researchers from other social science disciplines because they create an artificial social setting, but they can be useful for eliciting contrasting opinions on an issue of mutual interest to members of a group (such as debates about parliamentary elections, the US presidential campaign race, or the funding of public services, for example) (see, for instance, Barbour 2008; Bernard 1998).
- Questionnaires and surveys are similarly less common in anthropology than in the more quantitative social sciences, but can be an efficient way to gather a lot of background information relevant to your project (such as specific details about the cinema-going habits of your informants) (see, for example, Denscombe 2010; Ritchie and Lewis 2003; VanderStoep and Johnston 2009).
- Elicitation involves asking your participants to record specific aspects of their lives in photographs, videos, or diaries. Elicitation is not appropriate for all research projects (for example, busy workers might not be impressed if you ask them to keep a diary for them). Elicitation threatens to be expensive when it requires cameras, video cameras, or voice recorders, but such technology is increasingly available on smart phones (which are of course not prevalent in very many fieldwork sites). Visual material (whether elicited or provided by you) can be used to initiate conversations about the particular worldviews of your informants (see, for example, Harper 2002).
- Participatory and multimodal methods involve engaging your informants and collaborating in the generation of data and knowledge. These methods often entail visual communication and might involve making a map together, walking through a neighbourhood with a participant, or producing a collaborative art exhibition. Again, such methods often produce artificial social settings, but can usefully generate valuable insights within a relatively short timeframe. See Box 5.1 on page 80 for a description and some useful references.

A more detailed discussion about using some of these methods in the field, and the types of information they generate, can be found in Chapter 5.

Secondary research methods

Secondary research methods: the searching, evaluating and synthesizing of secondary information, are an indispensable part of the anthropologist's toolkit. If you wish to engage with scholarly literature, libraries, archives, newspapers, cultural artifacts, visual materials, websites, film and photographs, you will need to conduct some secondary research. Turn to the next chapter for advice about using secondary research methods as well as different ways to approach secondary sources.

Reflect on which methods might be most appropriate and practical for your project. You are likely to be expected to give an indication of your proposed methods in your research proposal, with the caveat that you will remain flexible and adapt your methods as appropriate once you are conducting research (see Chapter 5).

Key points

- Think imaginatively about the research methods available to you, and try to choose methods that will help you to gain insights on your research topic.
- Be flexible: your understanding of what methods are appropriate and revealing may be turned upside down by your actual experience of fieldwork.

Aside from her research at the funeral parlour, **Janet** was also interested in how undertakers engage with death in their lives beyond their work, in particular the marking of death with specific rituals. She had no intention of turning up uninvited at funerals, but hoped that after getting to know people she might be invited to participate in Catholic ceremonies celebrating the various stages of life and death – christenings, first communions, weddings, and funerals. She was disappointed that she would miss the annual Day of the Dead, but thought that her interest in the aesthetics of death might benefit from using photographs from previous Day of the Dead festivals. She thought she might use these during interviews to encourage people to tell her about their experiences of previous festivals and their preparations for the next festival.

John's local greyhound track held races three evenings every week throughout the summer months, so he decided that his fieldwork should encompass one full greyhound-racing season, getting to know the characters of the staff and regular attendees (as well as the dogs themselves). John was interested in the question of how someone decides what dog to bet money on, which he imagined might have a visual aspect. He could envisage standing at the greyhound dog pen and engaging in informal conversations with prospective punters telling him what physical attributes make up a good racing dog. John thought he might ask punters to take photographs to make a visual record of all of the dogs they bet on during one given evening for debrief after the event, when they might reflect differently on their choices depending on the success or failure of their chosen dogs in the races.

Ethical considerations

Ethical issues can arise at any stage in a research project – from planning, to research, to writing up. Chapter 6 discusses the relationship between anthropology and ethics in detail, as well as common ethical issues such as informed consent, anonymity and confidentiality. As you design your project you may need to address the ethical implications of your research project and undertake an ethical review procedure. In most cases you will also be expected to provide a thorough discussion of any ethical issues raised by your project in your research proposal.

The codes of ethics developed by professional bodies such as the Association of Social Anthropologists of the UK and Commonwealth (http://www.theasa.org/ethics.shtml) and the American Anthropological Association (http://www.aaanet.org/profdev/ethics) are available online, and you should consult these for guidance. Additionally, your department and university will have a particular ethics review procedure in place, and you should refer to this while planning your project. In most cases, particularly if you plan to carry out ethnographic fieldwork, you will need to complete an ethical review form or self-audit form, in collaboration with your project supervisor. The forms should be easily accessible from your departmental website or available from your supervisor. These processes are designed to help you anticipate and resolve any ethical or safety issues before embarking on your research. So, it is worth taking some time to reflect on your plans and read through the review questions in conjunction with the ethics chapter in this book. You cannot anticipate all ethical eventualities; ethics will be something you refer to and reflect upon throughout your research project.

The specific requirements will vary from country to country and university to university, but an initial ethical review or self-audit form will likely ask you to consider some combination of the following:

- Confidentiality and consent
  - How will you obtain the informed consent of your research participants and ensure that their anonymity is protected in your fieldnotes and subsequent outputs?
- Conflicts of interest
  - What is your motivation for doing this research? Has your objectivity been compromised by any vested interests in the outcome of your research?
  - If you are lucky enough to be offered funding, what is the funder's motivation for supporting your research? What, if anything, does the funder expect to get in return? Aside from your dissertation, what other uses might be made of your findings?

- Data protection
  - If your research entails the collection of sensitive data about specific individuals or institutions, how will you store this data securely, and who else (if anyone) will have access to the raw data?
- Risk management
  - What are the potential stresses, physical or psychological risks you might face, and what steps are you taking to minimize these risks?
  - Will you be working on sensitive topics and/or with vulnerable participants, and if so how will you protect them to prevent them from coming to any harm as a result of participating in your research?
- Responsibilities to others
  - What steps are you taking to ensure that your research project will not jeopardize the reputations of your university, your funding body, or the discipline of anthropology in general, and that your conduct during the research process will not threaten access or pose other problems for future researchers in your area?

If any significant risks or ethical problems are identified you will be asked to pass through a more detailed assessment procedure. Similarly, if you plan to conduct research in an unstable region, or to work with children or vulnerable adults, for example, a more detailed ethical or legal review may be required. In some cases a criminal background check may need to be carried out by external institutions. Think carefully about the ethical implications and feasibility of the research you intend to do. Checks take time, so try to plan ahead.

Key points

- Try to anticipate and address any ethical issues before embarking on research.
- Be aware that it is likely that your most serious ethical dilemmas have not yet revealed themselves to you, and will do so at some point during the research process (see Chapter 6).

While completing the ethical review form for her university department **Janet** realized that the topic of death and associated funerary activities raised several ethical issues for her research project. Observing activities at a funeral parlour and watching embalmers at work sounded macabre and exciting, but would it be ethical? How could a dead person consent to her presence? On the other hand, perhaps she would find the business of preparing bodies too depressing and stressful. When writing her research proposal and contacting funeral directors in Mexico, Janet explained that she was interested in the work of undertakers and their aesthetic decisions about how to prepare a body for burial. She stated clearly that this would involve talking to the undertakers working at the funeral parlour but that she would not seek to come into contact with the actual dead bodies or with the bereaved families themselves.

John was keen to find out more about gambling addiction and its treatments. He wanted to work with a gambling addiction organization, but after considering the ethical implications he had some concerns about anonymity and informed consent since gambling addiction is a sensitive issue, and people might wish to join treatment programmes anonymously. John's very presence at a private meeting would deny them this right. Instead, John decided that it would be less problematic to join an online gambling addiction discussion and support group, where anonymity could be guaranteed and participation in his project would always be responsive and not imposed upon anyone. He hoped that he might be able to persuade people to meet him in person after they had become familiarized with his project online.

Practical arrangements

Language proficiency

Language may not be a major issue for students who are planning a research project 'at home', or in other native language-speaking contexts or archives. However, language competency should be an important consideration if you want to conduct research amongst people who speak other languages or if you plan to work with archives in other languages. Early anthropologists in the field often worked with local translators, which is associated with myriad problems of translation and comprehension. In *Argonauts of the Western Pacific*, however, Bronislaw Malinowski (1922: 23) championed a more direct approach: the ethnographer 'who acquires a knowledge of the native language and can use it as an instrument of inquiry'. Anthropologists have never looked back: while the use of research assistants and translators is a common practice, by and large it is preferable for an ethnographer to speak the local language (or languages) in order to communicate more effectively with informants.

Your proficiency in the language or languages spoken by your research participants, or in which your research materials are recorded or written, will have a huge influence on your research experience and on the quality of your research data. Of course, if your specific research topic engages with language or linguistic issues – if you are looking at metaphors, rumours, and gossip, or illocutionary speech, for instance – then language will be of central importance. But, whatever the specific focus of your research, language will be relevant because so much social and political knowledge, communication, and practice is embedded in language. Language is central to the anthropological endeavour, and some anthropologists spend years learning new languages and dialects. Even much of the information we gather to do with embodied dispositions or the unspoken aspects of social and cultural life, is accessed or generated through asking and speaking about them. Thus, language is the medium of so much of what anthropologists do, both in terms of primary fieldwork and secondary or library-based research, and in terms of the final products of our labour: in your case, the dissertation and/or visual ouputs based on your research.

Especially at undergraduate or masters level, when you may have only a few months during the long vacation to complete your project, it does not make much sense to go somewhere where you do not speak or read the relevant language. You would be better off choosing a field site where you will be able to communicate with people and engage with secondary materials. If you speak only English, Arabic, or Portuguese, then your project will be more likely to succeed if you choose a field site where your informants communicate with one another in English, Arabic, or Portuguese. If you have lived and functioned in another language, or have studied languages at school or university, you may be in a position to choose a field site where your linguistic talents will come in handy. And, in the longer term, brushing up your language skills during your fieldwork will do no harm to your career prospects either.

If you would like to conduct fieldwork in another language but feel that your language skills are rusty, you have several options for getting practice before you leave. For instance:

- You may be able to take a language course alongside your anthropology courses in the academic year running up to your fieldwork. This option has several advantages: it will not cost you extra, it will expose you to the literature of your chosen language, and it might even contribute positively to your degree.
- Your university or the local council might offer short, part-time language courses as evening classes. A key advantage with this option is that you might be able to choose between courses that focus on comprehension and speaking (which would help you in fieldwork) or those that concentrate on reading and writing (which would be handy for archival work). On the other hand, such courses cost money and take time, which might make them incompatible with your degree course and other commitments.
- Websites offering films, visual clips, audio courses, and parallel texts provide an incredibly useful language resource for researchers. These online options also enable you to practise and develop your language skills across a range of listening, reading and speaking activities.
- You could also advertise on campus or online for mutual conversational practice sessions with international or exchange students (offering English or another language in exchange). You could use a language exchange website to link with a partner elsewhere in the world and use Skype to conduct your conversations. The advantages of this option are that it can be free and is likely to concentrate on comprehension and speaking (rather than reading and writing). On the other hand, this option may not be so useful if you are doing a library-based project, and it may be harder to maintain momentum with such an informal arrangement than it would be with a formal language course.

Key points

- Your research will be most productive and enjoyable if you can communicate effectively and directly with your research participants.

Having studied Spanish at school and spent a year living in Spain as a child, **Janet** spoke good Spanish, which would stand her in good stead in Mexico. She did not feel the need to take a refresher language course, but – realizing that the Spanish spoken in Mexico differs significantly from that spoken in Spain – she thought she would benefit from conversational practice with a Mexican or other Latin American Spanish speaker. Janet paired up with a Mexican student on a language exchange website and started conversational practice over Skype. She began watching Latin American films online and even found some clips of Mexican funeral customs on YouTube, which she used to prepare a phrasebook of key terms to use once she arrived in Mexico.

John planned to remain in the UK for his fieldwork, and did not envision any language difficulties.

Permission and contacts

If you would like to do your fieldwork abroad, check out visa requirements as soon as you have settled on your field site and make any necessary arrangements or applications in advance. If you plan to travel abroad, consult the travel advice provided by your country's government – the UK Foreign and Commonwealth Office website (www.fco.gov.uk) or US Department of State website (http://travel.state.gov) for example – which offer travel advice by country and advise on relevant risks and safety precautions. Reflect carefully about whether it is really worth risking your safety by trying to do your fieldwork in an unstable region – and in addition to concerns about your well-being, bear in mind that your travel insurance may be invalidated if you go against official advice to avoid certain areas.

Getting permission for your research is something that affects many but not all research projects. Regardless of which country you want to work in, different kinds of research projects require widely divergent degrees of engagement with authorities at various levels. If you plan to work in a very informal or public setting – at summer music festivals across Europe, or up mountains in Scotland, for example – you may not need to seek official permission at all, although you will still need to seek the informed consent of each of your prospective informants (see Chapter 6 for more on this). If, however, you plan to work in a more formal institutional or private setting – in a museum, mosque, factory, or café, for example – then you will need official permission from that institution's management. Applying for research permission in advance is always a good idea, but it is crucial if you hope to work in an even more tightly controlled environment – such as a scientific laboratory, a boarding school, a young offenders' detention centre, or a refugee camp – which might turn out to be impenetrable. If it might turn out that you are not going to be allowed to work there at all, then it's better to find this out in advance so that you can save your energies and adapt your proposed project. Applying for permission may involve a lot of negotiation with several layers of bureaucracy, so make a good impression from the start by behaving professionally and explaining your research project clearly. Once you have got the relevant permits, make additional copies of the paperwork to be stored in safe places (while carrying one copy with you).

Once you have got your visa and permit, it might seem simplest just to turn up unannounced at your proposed field site and hope that people will want to talk to you. But how would you salvage your project if you unknowingly turned up in a village in the middle of the harvest season so all the villagers were too busy to accommodate you or talk to you? And what would you do if the community leaders felt slighted by your failure to ask their permission first, and prevented other community members from engaging with you? On balance, it will be less stressful in the short term and more efficient in the long term to identify some key people with whom to discuss your plans – and, if necessary, to get permission for your study in advance.

Some tips for seeking permission and access:

- If you do not already have a pre-existing contact in your proposed field site, you might be able to use the internet, email and social networking sites to establish some key contacts in the field.
- Some institutions and communities may have so-called 'gatekeepers' who wield considerable influence over whether other members of the community will feel able engage with you, in which case you may have to seek the approval of the 'gatekeepers' in advance.
- You could consider whether you might benefit from being affiliated to a local institution (such as a university) during your fieldwork.
- It might be worth finding out if other researchers will be in the area at the same time, in which case you could meet and discuss your project with them.

Key points

- Try to organize visas, permits, permissions and contacts in advance of embarking upon fieldwork; not doing so could spell trouble for the viability of your research project.

Janet was worried about how she would persuade an undertaker to allow her to work behind the scenes at a funeral parlour, so she was keen to get permission arranged in advance. She had already searched online for a list of *funerarias* (funeral parlours) in Mexico and emailed the funeral directors, some of whom had written back to enquire about her project.

John knew that he could attend public events – like greyhound races – without requiring permission, but he also wanted to spend time at one of the greyhound training kennels, so he made contacts in advance and applied for a voluntary half-time administrative position at the kennel.

Budget and timetable

Preparation of a budget might not be crucial for fieldwork 'at home' or in the archives, but will be important particularly if your funds are limited or if you are applying for funding to support your research. Try to be realistic about the reasonable expenses likely to be associated with your project. A research budget is usually best presented in table format, and may include the following items of expenditure:

Table 2.1

Expense	Questions to consider
Visa	What kind of visa do you need, and how much does it cost for the length of your fieldwork?
Travel insurance	What would happen to you if you got sick or had an accident and needed to spend time in a hospital abroad? Are you sure that you could get home quickly if necessary in an emergency?
Travel to your field site	How will you get to your field site in the first place?
Travel during fieldwork	Can you get around on foot, will you use public transport, or will you buy or hire a vehicle?
Accommodation	Will you stay with family or friends (in which case, what contribution will you make?), or will you rent a room or an apartment? (See Chapter 5 for advice about living arrangements.)
Food	Will meals or cooking facilities be provided with your accommodation, or will you have to buy your meals ready-made?
Communications	How will you contact people in the field and at home? Do you have a mobile phone you can use in the field? Do you need frequent internet access?
Documents	Will you want to buy books, journals, or a daily newspaper to keep up to date with local news stories? Will you need to make large numbers of photocopies (for example, if you are working in the archives or producing survey questionnaires)?
Research assistance	Do you need anyone to help you with your research (for example, to introduce you to participants or to help you with focus groups or translation)?
Gifts for informants	What gifts from your home town or branded items from your university gift shop might be well received?

A timetable for research is something else that might be required for research proposals and funding applications (again, best in table format), but it is also something that can help you to keep tabs on your progress. As well as obliging you to think through your proposed activities, it also sets goals and deadlines for you to reach and breaks the overall project into a series of more manageable steps.

Table 2.2

Stage of research	Questions to consider
Preparation	Do you need to spend time refreshing your language skills before setting off for research?
	What secondary literature do you need to engage with before you begin research?
Research	What will you do as soon as you arrive in the field?
	How long will the initial settling-in phase take?
	What activities will make up the bulk of your primary fieldwork and/or secondary research, and how much time will they take?
	How long do you plan to be in the field or in the archives, and what is your justification for this being a sufficient length of time to carry out this project?
Analysis and writing	How long will it take to organize your research materials and analyze your fieldnotes?
	How much time should you set aside for engaging with secondary literature on your return from the field?
	How long will it take to write up your dissertation (bearing in mind that your time may be under pressure from starting new courses at university by then)?
	Where does the dissertation deadline fall within the academic year and in relation to other deadlines?

Key points

- Be realistic: a research project is likely to cost more and take longer than you might initially think.

Janet's single largest expense would be her flights to Mexico. She had organized to rent a room cheaply via her friends in Mexico, but once she calculated a daily rate for food and local travel, she realized how quickly her costs would mount up, and she estimated that her savings would be inadequate. She decided to apply to a foundation in her home town for additional funding, and received a small grant that covered her travel costs.

John would be returning home after the end of term, and would be living at home in exchange for small contributions to the household, so his living costs were not high. His research costs would be limited to bus travel to the greyhound track, entrance to greyhound races (he had decided not to give in to temptation to have the odd flutter on the races), and refreshments for research participants. John wanted to apply for work to help make ends meet, but was concerned about managing his time and making sure he was dedicating enough time and energy to his fieldwork, so he prepared himself a calendar. He marked the days he would be volunteering at the kennels and the evenings he would be at the greyhound race track, and he set aside a couple of hours each day for writing his fieldnotes. This left him with enough time for a part-time summer job, but he realized that he couldn't go back to the pub where he used to work because bartending entails weekend and evening shifts, whereas he would need to be at the greyhound track three evenings a week.

References

Agar, Michael. 1996. *The Professional Stranger: An Informal Introduction to Ethnography*. London: Academic Press.

Atkinson, Paul, Amanda Coffey, Sara Delamont, John Lofland and Lyn Lofland. 2001. *Handbook of Ethnography*. London: Sage.

Atkinson, Paul and Martyn Hammersley. 2007. *Ethnography: Principles in Practice*. 3rd edition. London: Routledge.

Barbash, Ilsa and Lucien Taylor. 1997. *Cross-Cultural Filmmaking: A Handbook for Making Documentary and Ethnographic Films and Videos*. Berkeley: University of California Press.

Barbour, Rosaline. 2008. *Doing Focus Groups*. London and New York: Sage.

Becker, Howard. 1998. *Tricks of the Trade: How to Think About Your Research While You're Doing It*. Chicago: University of Chicago Press.

Bernard, Russell H. (ed.) 1998. *Handbook of Methods in Cultural Anthropology*. Lanham, MD: AltaMira Press.

Blommaert, Jan. 2010. *Ethnographic Fieldwork: A Beginner's Guide*. Bristol: Multilingual Matters.

Denscombe, Martyn. 2010. *The Good Research Guide For Small Scale Social Research Projects*. 4th edition. Maidenhead: Open University Press.

DeWalt, Kathleen M. and Billie R. DeWalt. 2010. *Participant Observation: A Guide for fieldworkers*. 2nd edition. Maryland: Altamira Press.

Ferguson, James. 1990. *The Anti-Politics Machine: 'Development', Depoliticization, and Bureaucratic Power in Lesotho*. Cambridge: Cambridge University Press.

Harper, Douglas. 2002. 'Talking About Pictures: A Case for Photo Elicitation', *Visual Studies*, 11 (1): 13–26.

Imel, Susan. 2011. 'Writing a Literature Review'. In T. S. Rocco and T. Hatcher (eds), *The Handbook of Scholarly Writing and Publishing*. San Francisco: Jossey-Bass, pp. 145–60.

Malinowski, Bronislaw. 1922. *Argonauts of the Western Pacific: An Account of Native Enterprise and Adventure in the Archipelagoes of Melanesian New Guinea*. London: Routledge.

Messick, Brinkley. 1993. *The Calligraphic State: Textual Domination and History in a Muslim Society*. Cambridge: Cambridge University Press.

Miller, Daniel. 1994. *Modernity, An Ethnographic Approach: Dualism and Mass Consumption in Trinidad*. Oxford: Berg.

Okely, Judith. 2011. *Anthropological Practice: Fieldwork and the Ethnographic Method*. London: Berg.

Pink, Sarah. 2007 (2001). *Doing Visual Ethnography*. London: Sage.

——2012. *Advances in Visual Methodology*. London: Sage.

Ritchie, Jane and Jane Lewis (eds). 2003. *Qualitative Research Practice: A Guide for Social Science Students and Researchers*. London: Sage.

Rose, Gillian. 2011. *Visual Methodologies: An Introduction to Researching with Visual Materials*. London: Sage.

VanderStoep, Scott W. and Deidre D. Johnston (eds). 2009. *Research Methods for Everyday Life: Blending Qualitative and Quantitative Approaches*. San Francisco: Jossey-Bass.

Wacquant, Loïc. 2002. 'Scrutinizing the Street: Poverty, Morality, and the Pitfalls of Urban Ethnography', *American Journal of Sociology*, 107(6): 1468–1532.

Watson, C. W. (ed.) 1999. *Being There: Fieldwork in Anthropology (Anthropology, Culture and Society)*. London: Pluto Press.

Wilson, Richard. 2001. *The Politics of Truth and Reconciliation in South Africa: Legitimizing the Post-Apartheid State*. Cambridge: Cambridge University Press.

3   On the primary importance of secondary research

Neil Thin

'Secondary research' is a catch-all term meaning re-examination of information which has been gathered for other purposes. You may do this using 'primary sources' (first-hand information), 'secondary sources' (information others
have derived from primary sources), or 'tertiary sources' (meta-analysis of
several secondary sources). Anthropological research projects tend to rely on
secondary research at every stage, including during 'fieldwork'. Too many
researchers give secondary research only second-rate consideration. This is a
mistake. Anthropologists have always tended to learn a great deal more from
indirect media such as archives, libraries, the web, newspapers, cultural artifacts, and film than they do from 'primary' face-to-face sources. Secondary
research is becoming still more important as the internet becomes our main
source of information (academic and non-academic, verbal and non-verbal).
Secondary research requires careful planning while also itself providing key
inputs into the planning process. You must think laterally about what your key
search terms might be, what the most useful and efficient information sources
will be, how to achieve a reasonably diverse and unbiased portfolio of sources, and how to organize the information so that a viable and valid research
story emerges from it. Developing these capabilities and habits will not only
help your dissertation but will help you develop crucial life skills in learning
from and communicating with multiple sources in many places.

Not by primary fieldwork alone: varieties of research and sources

Anthropological research is all about fieldwork, right? And fieldwork is all
about primary face-to-face learning, isn't it? Wrong on both counts. As in
other social sciences, it is *secondary* research that anthropologists spend most of
their time on. And even in 'the field' (if we have a main research site) it may
well turn out that much of our research isn't direct learning from observation
and talking, but secondary use of information that others have gathered. In a
sense, all research is secondary, since the term 'research' itself means generating
knowledge by looking *again* through information.

Research information is 'primary' if it is gathered directly through first-hand
experience. In anthropology, this usually means observing people and their
environments, and engaging them in conversations. It is 'secondary' if new uses

and analysis are added to data that were collected for different purposes, usually by different researchers. For anthropologists the primary/secondary distinction is blurred, since many anthropologists throughout their careers revisit their primary research information and apply it to very different research questions from those originally asked. Also, even in 'the field' we typically conduct secondary research if we, for example, borrow people's diaries or glance through records of their meetings or read the accounts of local historians.

Secondary research information is usually gleaned from media hosts such as archives, libraries, the web, newspapers, cultural artifacts, and film rather than from 'primary' face-to-face sources (although note that internet ethnography can also be 'primary' if the researcher is interacting with people online, as for example, in research on cyber-relationships). Figure 3.1 illustrates how the (loose) distinctions between direct and indirect learning, and between onsite and offsite learning, help us to identify four main categories of learning that inform our research, of which 'primary fieldwork' is only one.

So our main information sources throughout our careers and through every stage of research are compiled by other people, mainly in the form of written

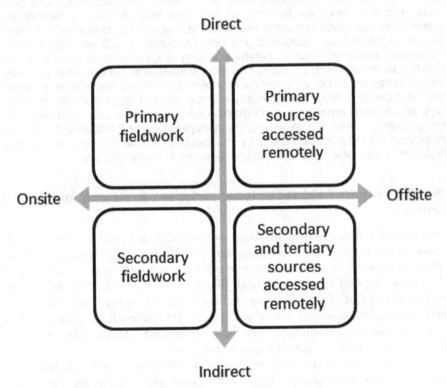

Figure 3.1 Primary and secondary research.

texts, verbal scripts or stories, or visual products. It is embarrassingly common for ethnographic monographs and textbooks on 'ethnography' or even on 'qualitative research' to ignore secondary research methods and implicitly assume that all important 'data' are 'primary'. Partly this derives from the confusing but very common habit of using 'ethnography' as shorthand for 'fieldwork'. This is a residue from earlier strategic efforts to distinguish this from 'ethnological' research that was based on 'second-hand' accounts of travellers and missionaries.

Despite the salience of primary fieldwork in the professional identity of anthropologists, many key ethnographic texts have been based entirely on secondary research. One of the most famous and widely read ethnographies of all time, Ruth Benedict's *The Crysanthemum and the Sword* (1989), was developed entirely from several layers of non-primary data, since Benedict had never even been to Japan, let alone collected any primary data there. Similarly, anthropology's two most famous essays, Mauss's 'Essay on the Gift' and Sahlins's 'Notes on the Original Affluent Society,' were based on secondary analysis of a few ethnographic accounts. The results of these texts were stimulating and they greatly enriched theoretical debates. Unfortunately, in all three cases their non-scientific, opinionated, piecemeal approach to selection of data detracts from their plausibility as scholarly contributions to knowledge. But the rise of historical anthropology since the 1950s has long established the importance of secondary research (both oral and written) for anthropologists (Brettell 1998).

Key points

- 'Ethnography' is not just fieldwork: considered broadly as the whole process of ethnographic research, it is more substantially informed by 'secondary' than by 'primary' information.
- Secondary research is an integral part of all stages of research, not just a separate one-off 'literature review'.

Why does secondary research matter?

In anthropology, all our learning is interconnected (De Munck 2009: vii). So primary fieldwork (if we do it at all) must always be inspired and informed by what we have learned from other sources. If the heart of ethnography is the study of 'everyday life' (Pawluch et al. 2005), and if people's everyday domestic and public lives worldwide are increasingly happening and being represented online, it follows that a large and increasing portion of our ethnographic research must be based on secondary information that is available to researchers online. Similarly, as organizational realities, relationships, and policies are taking textual form and increasingly becoming multi-sited, ethnographies of these must rely mainly on secondary sources and indirect communication (Abram 2003).

Among the many reasons why a robust secondary research strategy might be seen as even more important in anthropology than in other social sciences, three stand out. First, an emphasis on *holism* means that being receptive to a wide variety of kinds and sources of information is the hallmark of the anthropologist, both in the field and on campus. Second, cross-cultural *comparison* means that all anthropological research should involve synthesizing knowledge from diverse sources – from different places, different people and different disciplines. At a bare minimum we must use secondary information to provide some kind of comparative backdrop to whatever we are writing about. Third, most anthropologists favour iterative, multistranded, labyrinthine research that is flexible and open to surprises, in contrast to the more rigidly linear 'tramline' research that positivist science favours; secondary research helps us draw together links between multiple lines of enquiry.

Sometimes disparaged in the past as 'armchair' anthropology and labelled 'ethnology' as distinct from 'ethnography', secondary research doesn't dispense with informants, it's just that the informants provide us their knowledge indirectly, in a form that has to some extent already been selected, gathered and analyzed for other purposes.

Box 3.1

Uses you might make of secondary sources

- Inspiration to help you identify suitable topics.
- Generating a list of hypotheses and research questions.
- Definitions of relevant key concepts.
- Guidance on methods and approaches to similar topics.
- Sources of key references.
- Collecting background information on historical, geographical, demographic, cultural, or political issues (for use not only in proposals and dissertations, but also during fieldwork as a basis for conversations and further enquiries).
- Using audio, visual and audio-visual information (sound clips, photos, artwork, video clips) to help familiarize you with settings and events.
- Inspiration on writing styles, use of graphics and approaches to structuring.
- Strengthening your proficiency in local language or dialect, particularly your ability to converse on your research themes.
- As a starting-point for internet-mediated primary research, e.g. seeking out informants through interest groups and online volunteer surveys (see Hewson et al., 2003: ch. 3).

Secondary sources are important not only for the information that they deliver directly, but also more indirectly for what they reveal about the cultural processes and institutions they are associated with. Anthropologists study *in* archives for their contents, but they also *study archival processes* as a way of learning about what people see as important and about how they organize and remember information. Since an archive is never an unproblematic source of information we need to explore the processes of archivization for what they tell us about bureaucracy, governance, salience and deliberate remembering.

Key points

- We will only know what kind of primary information to look for, why it might matter, and what it might mean, if our secondary research is adequate.
- Secondary sources are interesting objects of ethnographic analysis, not just useful repositories of information.

Making your secondary research efficient, systematic and transparent

In many social research fields, most commonly in health and educational research, the term 'systematic review' has gained currency as a concept for approaches to secondary sources that are sufficiently robust and transparent to be replicable by others and to minimize the risk of biased findings (Booth 2001). Systematic reviews divide into those emphasizing *quantitative* approaches (commonly known as 'meta-analysis'), and those emphasizing *qualitative* and interpretive approaches (known as 'meta-ethnography', see e.g. Doyle 2003; Britten and Pope 2012). Sometimes 'meta-analysis' (synthesizing several studies which had similar objectives or hypotheses) is distinguished from 'secondary analysis' (drawing out new understandings from information originally gathered for different purposes).

None of these concepts has gained currency in anthropology. If anthropologists are notoriously reticent or vague about their approaches to managing fieldwork-based primary information, most are even more reluctant to divulge the secrets of their secondary research. Where librarians and scientistically minded researchers emphasize rational and efficient systems for searching, evaluating, sorting and analyzing secondary sources, most anthropologists are uncomfortable with the idea of rule-governed secondary research, and instead embrace the increasingly chaotic and volatile variety of secondary information with the same individualistic optimism that they approach the diversity of information in the field. As Atkinson and Hammersley have argued (2007: 3), all ethnographic data collection must be relatively unstructured since the interpretive categories emerge from the data rather than being specified in advance.

This relatively *ad hoc* approach often serves us very well, increasing our chances of making serendipitous linkages and surprising synergies between different information sources. Without any scientific system we can of course make no pretence of producing replicable or non-tendentious findings, but for many anthropologists this is no disadvantage. In our defence, we can point not only to the many advantages of fluid and idiosyncratic research, but also to the under-acknowledged biases that derive from being hide-bound by the conventional protocols of 'systematic review'. Obsessive systematization and efficiency risk losing us the benefits of flexible, iterative learning and of attending to a rich multiplicity of information sources.

Still, while recognizing this trade-off between systematicity and flexibility, a reasonable minimum requirement is that we are systematic enough to be both efficient and transparent. You need to be able to declare and justify your choices of information sources – what you looked for, what you gave most attention to, and why. Remember to note which archives or databases you searched, using which terms and restrictions (e.g. in title and keyword fields only), and covering which periods. If you forget any of these details, you may find yourself either wasting time on repeat searches or, worse, misrepresenting your information sources when you write up. You may also want to develop a documents archive, plus an associated bibliographic database and collection of notes on specific items as well as cross-cutting themes and patterns.

Rules for scholarly transparency may be formally set out for you as part of a 'literature review' requirement. Even if not, your discussion of 'methods' and your account of how your research themes and arguments developed should also include explanation of how you made use of secondary research. Although many guide books on dissertations more or less assume that you will write a separate literature review chapter, this isn't always a good idea. It is more important to ensure that your whole text engages well with secondary sources, showing at every turn that you are drawing inspiration and information from a rich variety of other knowledge sources.

By being moderately systematic, you will strengthen rather than inhibit flexibility and comprehensiveness. You will ensure that your time use is optimal and that throughout the process you are consciously developing analytical storylines that justify the attention you give to diverse information sources. You must show clear evidence of how your research developed through engagement with the work of other knowledge producers – be they village orators, casual acquaintances, researchers, journalists, archivists, or museum curators.

To do so requires you to apply different *evaluative criteria* to your information sources, depending on your purposes. If you need accurate statistics, you will need to be able to evaluate the reliability of your sources of statistics (e.g. a government department or a commercial consultancy or an independent research team) and of any secondary interpretations of these statistics (journalists, businesses and government departments are often willfully irresponsible in their misinterpretations of statistics). If you're looking for scholarly works, you must be able to distinguish rigorous scholarship from sloppy pseudo-scholarship. If you need to get a range of opinions from different kinds of people, you need to find some way of ensuring that your particular search strategies or tools don't unduly bias the kinds of people from whom you get the information.

Nowadays, most researchers rely mainly but not solely on electronic resources for their secondary information. While accessing information has become unimaginably easier than it was a generation ago, the consequent data deluge puts enormous bureaucratic and psychological strains on researchers. The crucial thing to bear in mind is that although online resources enable us to become ever more efficient at accessing huge amounts of relevant information, efficient access is not the same thing as efficient use. Your aim, remember, is to do some original thinking and communicating on a topic that you find stimulating, not just to become just another node in the information network. E-texts are a very useful means but you mustn't let them ensnare you into information overload which can quickly cause confusion, worry and loss of motivation.

It is helpful to think of two quite different advantages that the internet offers to researchers. It facilitates *comprehensiveness* but can also enable *specialization*. On the one hand, the quick access to lots of relevant information enables you to be much broader and more inclusive in terms of the topics and disciplines you can engage with. On the other hand, clever online searches allow intelligent narrowing down of your topic towards much more precise, specific kinds of knowledge than would have been the case in the pre-internet era. If you allow yourself to become too easily seduced by the opportunity to read a huge range of texts, you may miss the opportunity to engage in more detail with a few authors specializing in your particular theme. Conversely, some internet searchers miss out on comprehensiveness, interdisciplinarity and serendipity by being too eager to use the power of the web for locating a few specialist items.

Box 3.2

Questions on conducting and presenting secondary research

- **Explaining your system and its rationale**
  In what ways was your gathering, sorting and analysis of secondary information systematic or strategic? What key terms guided your searches? How did these change and why? On what basis did you decide how to prioritize among your various information options? Which sources most influenced your research and how? Have you any advice for future researchers pursuing similar themes?

- **Developing a research narrative**
  Are you able to relate some kind of narrative or analytical story line about trends and patterns in the secondary sources you are

summarizing, to make it more engaging? If so, can you give a plausible account of how you arrived at this narrative through systematic rather than haphazard enquiry? How did the search of secondary information evolve as the research proceeded? Were there unexpected shifts of attention towards new themes that emerged?

- **Being transparent about the details of your system**
  To the extent that there was a system, is it presented with sufficient transparency and detail for readers to get a clear sense of how it was conducted, and draw their own conclusions as to its scientific rigour and representativeness? Is it clear which databases you consulted, when, and with what search terms and inclusion/exclusion criteria? Is it clear how you prioritized different kinds of information sources and how you selected some sources for more attention than others?

- **Explaining and justifying casualness and flexibility**
  Have you given plausible justifications for adopting a relatively loose, *ad hoc* approach to some of your secondary sources? What were the main influences on your searching process – your own intuition? Chance findings? Preference for reading academic anthropological texts? Regional preferences? English language publications? What kinds of bias or information shortfall should be acknowledged when drawing general conclusions from your review of secondary information? Could some of these factors have biased your findings?

- **Justifying uses of quotes and references**
  When you use full quotations rather than paraphrasing, is this justified by the originality, complexity, or intrinsic interest of the quotation? If so, does your commentary on the quotation show adequate engagement and add value to it? When you include references to texts without quoting from them, is it clear why you are referencing and what the text reference has to say on the matter at hand? (n.b. you will NOT improve your mark by listing multiple references without commenting on them, even though this dreadful habit is common in professional academic writing).

- **Generalizing**
  When drawing synthetic generalizations from the literature you have seen, have you clearly discussed the likely biases such as publication bias (e.g. towards 'positive' or remarkable findings), source bias (e.g. more studies from some regions or relating to particular kinds of population), and informant bias (people with particular kinds of opinion tending to volunteer information, or people tending to volunteer some kinds of information but not others)?

Key points

- Research projects will be more enjoyable and efficient, and their results more scientifically plausible, if you develop and explain a clear *system* for accessing, sorting and digesting secondary information, and base this on clear identification of the various *purposes* of secondary research.
- The need for a systematic and transparent methodology applies equally to primary and secondary research.
- Since anthropologists tend to be either unsystematic or non-transparent in their secondary research you should look to other social sciences for inspiration on how to be systematic and transparent in your use of secondary information.

Making it memorable and enjoyable

When you do primary or secondary research, you are engaging creatively with the world in rewarding ways. Primary research may seem more adventurous and glamorous, but secondary research can be equally rewarding. If you are well organized but also open to surprises, you will enhance the enjoyment while also giving yourself the best chance of being creative and of remembering what you are learning. For most people, enjoyment requires a sense that you are making progress. So it is crucial to keep thinking about the research narrative, highlighting the particular contributions that secondary research is making to your work.

How much use you make of secondary information, and what kinds of information you use, will depend on your own preferences, on requirements set by the academic department to which you are submitting, on the originality and scope of your themes, and on how well you do at gathering, sorting and making sense of relevant primary information. Nearly all academic departments will require substantial use of secondary information but they may or may not specify that this will account for part of your grade, and they may or may not require you to focus partly on primary research.

Skim-reading large numbers of texts (sometimes just tables of contents and abstracts, and perhaps introductory paragraphs and conclusions) is a powerful way of getting a quick sense of the diversity of disciplines and approaches relating to your topic. At this point you can just note down themes, ideas and any intriguing terms and concepts that might be worth exploring further. In this early stage you have the freedom to explore a few tangential themes that may or may not develop into more substantial avenues of research. This is exciting but can't be allowed to run on for too long.

Memorable and deep learning needs to be more engaged, with enough interaction for you to remember the important readings and be able to find them again. Soon you need to immerse yourself fully in some key texts, and follow this up with substantial noting of not just the key points but also your thoughts on how you might critique or build on their ideas. Remember that you are required not just to 'cover' a large amount of relevant literature, but also to synthesize and integrate what you've learned from this in creative ways, so that you become the originator of new knowledge (Imel 2011: 46–47).

Another helpful way of remembering key texts is to find out more about their authors: what discipline they work in, what research projects led to their publications, what research institute they work at, what they look like, who they have collaborated with, and what their other key works are. Fortunately, nowadays you can get all of this kind of information in a matter of seconds from the web, whereas a couple of decades ago it might have taken you months to find out.

You can also sustain both efficiency and motivation by thinking about what functions your secondary information will perform at different points of the research process. In the start-up phase, it can help you to guide initial planning and narrowing down the themes. It can also help you to develop a viable set of questions, and choose the most suitable method for finding answers to these, as well as identifying the variety of people to ask. In the field, sharing and cross-checking what you have learned from secondary research can be a really stimulating way of engaging people in conversation, while at the same time convincing potential sceptics of your scholarly integrity. Just as anthropologists are supposed to become fluent in the language of the people they are studying, so we must also try to become conversant with information and concepts relevant to our research places and themes: local history and geography, religious doctrine, comparative information on similar themes and activities in other places, etc.

If nothing else, an efficient early phase of research in which you gather and organize lots of relevant information and begin converting this into knowledge will give you confidence that even if your field research phase doesn't go well, you will still have enough data to compose a viable dissertation. Don't underestimate the importance of this as a way of keeping the fear of failure at bay and, more positively, building up your confidence as a knowledgeable expert in your chosen topics. Later, you may start to think about how secondary information will complement and enrich primary data when you come to present evidence in support of your overall arguments.

Getting started with secondary research

To use secondary sources well, you need to think about functions, sequencing and prioritizing. You will need to know what kinds of topics and questions you want information about, and develop a viable set of search terms and/or questions. But these will change in light of the information you come across. You need to appreciate the variety of possible kinds of information type (books, articles, official reports, personal diaries, photographs, drawings, oral texts, etc.) and think about where to look for these (online databases, websites of official agencies, libraries, local archives, museums, etc.). The more carefully you narrow down your themes, the more comprehensive you can be in your coverage. Some guidance texts on literature reviews advise you to try to find 'all relevant' texts; this is clearly always impossible, and obsessive attempts at comprehensive coverage will lead to serious frustration and loss of nerve. But you must try to look at a fairly representative sample of the most relevant literature without major gaps or biases.

Before starting your searching or browsing, or even just an enquiry with an expert for guidance, you should have drafted the following:

- **At least a preliminary sketch of your research themes, questions and purposes** (do a quick brainstorm to identify main themes and sub-themes, and perhaps map these out to show overlaps and hierarchical relationships; bear in mind that these are bound to change in response to secondary research).
- **A list of key terms and phrases** (use encyclopedias, dictionaries, thesauruses, the indexes of introductory textbooks, to develop this list).
- **A list of promising information sources:** databases, journals, authors, etc., which will serve not only as information sources but will also give you ideas for further refining and adapting your definitions of key terms and research questions (and when doing so try to prioritize, and also think about complementarities, overlaps and shared biases among these – making sure, for example, you aren't unduly biased towards government agencies, rich–country scholars, or for-profit corporate information sources).

Without such preparatory work, you risk quickly becoming inundated with references and information before you've devoted enough attention to your research rationales and priorities. Next, consider doing each of the following in the early stages of your research project:

- **Seek advice from information experts**
  A professional information scientist (probably available in your university library) should be able to give you much better guidance on your searching strategies than your supervisor could offer. They can advise you on generic skills such as keyword searches, website evaluation and software for analysis and storage. They will need you to give them a realistic steer regarding your thematic and geographical interests and purposes. Also consult your university's online guidance on e-research and library research, or look at the Open University SAFARI guide (http://www.open.ac.uk/safari) and at the Virtual Training Suite (http://www.vtstutorials.co.uk).
- **Draft a prioritized calendar of activities (see also Chapter 2)**
  Draw up a provisional calendar of dissertation project work with a to-do list, thinking about realistic timings and rational sequencing, and leaving ample time for missed interim deadlines and for addressing unanticipated issues – e.g. the goldmines of relevant secondary sources you may chance upon.
- **Choose and familiarize yourself with software tools**
  Consider whether your information database is going to become sufficiently complex to benefit from the help of bibliographic software such as Endnote,

Reference Manager, or Procite. Also consider whether you may want to use online bibliographic and information search aides such as CiteUlike (for website organizing and networking); Delicious (for 'social bookmarking', i.e. sharing collections of tagged and annotated website bookmarks); or Google Reader (for RSS newsfeeds). Although early adoption of these could save you a huge amount of time in later writing up stages, do bear in mind that for a short and fairly simple project it may be more efficient just to organize your notes well in a single word-processor file. If you are only going to use 50 references and consult a further 100 or so, you won't need complex database software.

- **Start sharing tasks with others**
  Social networking (e.g. Facebook, academia.edu) and social bookmarking (e.g. www.delicious.com) can quickly allow you to cooperate with other scholars working on related themes. RSS readers and Twitter are other helpful tools for ongoing information-sharing.

- **Get started with a quick reading list**
  This can be quickly gleaned from course lists (search under 'syllabus'), a supervisor's suggestions, an anthropology encyclopedia, Wikipedia, or the bibliography at the end of a key text. At first, just compile enough to help you think about which themes and sources are likely to become priorities.

- **Start mapping key trends, theories and debates**
  This will give you essential information for your research proposal and/or introductory dissertation chapter, while also helping you identify themes and search terms for more detailed exploration later. As you explore the various organizations and sites that you have identified as key information sources, note links among these – such as collaborations, citations and disagreements, and note any patterned contrasts between different regions or disciplines in their treatment of the topics you are interested in.

- **Note other researchers' methods**
  Take notes on relevant methods and methodological issues discussed in all the texts you look at, even if there is little or no explicit discussion of methods. Understanding methods is crucial both to your evaluation of the information sources and to conducting your own research.

- **Note options for tangential follow-up**
  When you come across interesting items, note journal sources, library section codes, websites and key references that you may find time to follow up later.

Janet does some quick web searching under 'funeral AND Mexico' and quickly glances through hundreds of texts (both scholarly and non-scholarly), images, and videos. She deliberately doesn't keep detailed notes at this point, leaving for later the more careful tasks of planning and documenting her searches and building a project archive. But she does note down useful phrases and synonyms for future searches, and jots down ideas that may be worth exploring – including looking at how Mexican funeral customs are adapted in other countries, at visual dimensions of public religious ceremonies, and at the texts of funeral prayers and eulogies. Doing this she quickly becomes aware that to write holistically about funerals she will need to study not only the anthropology of death and dying, but also information on kinship, religion, ritual, cosmology, bereavement, oratory and visual aesthetics. To get a sense of how this diversity of information can be managed, she carefully reads three ethnographic accounts of funerals in different countries.

John searches on '(betting OR gambling) AND greyhound' and finds copious information about how to bet on greyhounds, a smaller amount on the history of greyhound-racing, but little sign of relevant social science. He quickly realizes that he needs to think carefully about whether his main research interest is the gambling or the greyhound-racing. His core interest is in the gambling, but links from greyhound-racing blogs and websites make him aware that since gambling on non-human animal performance is a distinct subcategory of betting it will be interesting to explore literature on other manifestations of this, such as pigeon-racing, cockfighting and badger-baiting.This leads to further tangential searches on animal symbolism and the use of animals in augury. Turning back to gambling, he explores some blogs and help sites relating to gambling addiction, and begins to piece together a provisional analytical storyline linking uncertainty, addiction, escapism and human–animal relations.

Box 3.3

Kinds of information sources

- **Thematic and/or discipline-specific**
  Meta-analyses and critical review articles on relevant key themes – e.g. in review journals such as *Annual Review of Anthropology*; encyclopedias; introductory chapters; Ph.D. dissertations; discipline-based or thematic wikis and discussion groups (see the anthropology websites listed on the companion site to this book); conference sites, some of which offer full text papers; policy briefs, periodic reviews or thematic reports by relevant global agencies (UN agencies, World Bank, governmental or non-governmental development agencies, regional or thematic research institutes).

- **Location-specific**
  People's diaries; local newsletters; local archives such as genealogical records, local history and records of mortality and morbidity; legal or para-legal records; organizational archives; maps; private or public photographic or artistic exhibitions; socio-economic statistics; museum collections; basic statistical, geographic, political and cultural information on the country (e.g. national government websites, CIA fact files).

- **Generic sites, search tools and databases**
  Library catalogues (see the general social science websites listed on the companion website); newspapers (probably best to use an RSS feeder to access these); indexes to periodical literature (e.g. Social Science Citation Index, International Development Abstracts); official government sites with information on history, policies, research, demography etc. (but always bear in mind the likely biases of any kind of agency).

- **Academic E-texts**
  Accessible through your library catalogue or online sites offering full or partial full text access to books (Google Books, Amazon, Project Gutenberg) and journal articles (Anthrosource).
- **'Grey literature'**
  Information not fully in the public domain but often produced for training or conferences run by and for official bodies, and available in organizational archives.
- **Thematic collections of quotations**
  In a dictionary of quotations or online. (Note that online quotation databases often don't give accurate sources, but Google or Google Scholar should be able to help you identify the source of most good quotations.)
- **Cyber-research and research on cybersociality**
  Exploring online 'second life' personas, social networks, cyberinstitutions and trends in the flow of knowledge and attitudes through the internet (see e.g. Kozinets 2010; Whitehead and Wesch 2012).
- **Collections of visual and audio information**
  Maps; photos; videos; diagrams; drawing; artifacts (Flickr, Google Images, YouTube, iTunes).
- **Statistics**
  If you find yourself using vague quantifiers like 'many', 'more', 'increasingly,' or 'most', you might consider overcoming the numerophobic culture of anthropology and start using numbers.
- **Texts on secondary research**
  Find these by using the following search terms: 'literature review'; 'online searching'; 'search strategies'; 'data archives'; meta-analysis; meta-ethnography; 'systematic review'. Try narrowing searches down to anthropological literature using a qualifier like 'AND (anthropol★ OR ethnograph★ OR cross-cultural)'.

Next steps in the process of using secondary sources

The variety of stages in your secondary research will depend on how much time you allocate to it. Before spending any significant time on any text or site, you will need to think carefully about how you expect it will help you towards successful completion of your project, and (therefore) how long you ideally would like to spend on it. If in doubt, skim-read quickly through contents, introductory paragraphs, and index before deciding whether to spend any more time on it. If most of this is either irrelevant, obscure, or telling you stuff you already know, move quickly on to something else. Note any salient or potentially interesting general findings from searches – e.g. apparent trends in research or news, biases or attention deficits in particular disciplines.

You might want to consider the following different degrees and kinds of engagement with secondary information:

- Conduct some preliminary searches to get a quick sense of the amounts, qualities and sources of published material already available.
- Do a database search (e.g. Anthrosource, Google Scholar, Searcher) using keywords (singly or in combination).
- Do a citation-based search, starting with a highly relevant key text, and following links to texts that cite it.
- Use preliminary searches to refine or otherwise modify research themes, objectives and questions, and/or to refine further searches.
- Use information from preliminary searches to identify key sources for more careful attention – e.g. the most relevant authors, research teams or institutes, websites, journals.
- Use information from preliminary searches to develop a longer and/or better, more carefully prioritized and targeted set of terms for further searches.

Stages or levels of active reading and note-taking

Every researcher recognizes the risks, increasing all the time, of spending too high a proportion of your secondary research time collecting and sorting readings rather than reading, and too much time reading rather than thinking about and responding to the readings. You can increase your chances of avoiding these frustrations and inefficiencies by considering carefully the different *levels* at which you can engage with secondary sources:

- Identifying, accessing and collecting texts (perhaps starting with the most recent first, using these to track backwards to the most seminal earlier texts), and maintaining a system for sorting and coding basic bibliographic references.
- Skim-reading to identify the most promising texts and parts of texts, and to develop a general sense of common themes and patterns in the research.
- Thorough reading of a much smaller set of readings identified as both high quality and of strong relevance, and maintaining a system for sorting and coding notes (brief summaries, fuller paraphrases and quotations, critical commentaries and creative responses) on readings.
- Reading and noting reviews of the most important books, and commentaries on the most important articles, plus drafting your own responses to these.
- Writing and sorting fully discursive text (at least full paragraphs, and perhaps also analytical diagrams) on readings that can form part of your own dissertation text.

If you proceed too hastily to deep reading and engaged interactions with texts, then unless you've been very clever or lucky at finding the most relevant texts you will spend too long on a few readings and miss a lot of more important potential readings. If you spend too long looking for ideal readings and collecting bibliographic information, you'll be frustrated when you come to write up and see how little time is left to make use of the readings you've identified.

Some practical considerations

- **Academic advice versus guidance on information skills**
  Your academic supervisors, particularly if they are anthropologists, may be far less suitable than librarians as sources of advice on searching and information management. Make an appointment with a librarian or information advisor early on in your research, and check what generic guidance is available to you on library and online resources. Also use your favourite search engine (e.g. Google, AltaVista, Lycos) to consult some simple generic guidance texts on dissertation preparation – e.g. searching 'dissertation writing' or 'dissertation research', or just look at some of the sites in the further reading list on the companion website.

- **Archiving and sorting secondary information**
  Nowadays, on just about any topic you will quickly find more information than you can possibly remember or use. You face tricky juggling acts between gathering, sorting and using information. Too much gathering without careful sorting, and you'll suffer from chaotic information overload and fail to make good use of what you've gathered. But obsessive sorting will eat into time that might be better spent on creative engagement with secondary information. For a short dissertation project a simple note filing with keyword tagging will suffice, though for large amounts of information some reference management software and/or qualitative data analysis software would help (see Chapter 7).

- **Recording your online searches**
  Though this may seem less essential than noting the texts and information that you find, it is also important to keep track of what searches you have done and where – which search tools sites and databases you made use of, what search tools you used, at what date. This matters for your own efficiency (you don't want to confuse yourself or waste time with duplicate searches), but also for the sake of giving a transparent account of how you arrived at your findings.

- **Accessing information while in the field**
  Nowadays, most fieldworkers will be able to take a laptop, and in most locations you won't be too far away from an internet connection. Still, it's worth thinking about when and where you might want to be able to access any crucial background information you may have gathered before embarking on fieldwork. Also consider carefully where you will do your online searching from. Many of the excellent resources you have free access to on-campus will not be available to you off-campus, so if you will be off-campus for a long spell you will probably need to build in an initial on-campus phase during which you download copies of texts which you are likely to want to read.

- **Access to local archives and other information sources**
  Sometimes it can take a while to locate the people and secure the permission to access local archives, so you may want to start negotiating access before you embark on fieldwork.
- **Using secondary sources during fieldwork**
  It is rather obvious that good fieldwork depends heavily on substantial preparatory work such as becoming familiar with existing information on your chosen themes, places and organizations, and with the local language. Less obviously, you may benefit greatly by using secondary sources to stimulate conversations during fieldwork. For example, you could build up a collection of key quotes or anecdotes, or an audio-visual archive (sound clips, photos, videos) that can be used both as conversational prompts during field research, and later in facilitating writing up, and in presentations.
- **Sharing information and tasks**
  Anthropologists tend to perceive themselves as working alone, and collaborative dissertation work is much rarer in anthropology departments than it is in other social sciences such as psychology (see Matsutake Worlds Research Group, 2009). But do you really want to work alone? Why not find other social scientists, or perhaps natural scientists, who might be anywhere in the world, with whom to collaborate for at least part of your work? Linking up with students at other universities may be particularly useful for specialist research where your own university may not give you access to all the books and journals you need. Online collaboration is much easier now than ever before, via email, social networking and social bookmarking sites. If you are going to share information and tasks systematically, you'll want to agree on how to do this. Do, however, check your institution's rules on what kinds of collaboration are allowed for assessed work.

Key points

- To be in command of your secondary research you need a clear sense of how and why you are choosing among a wide range of information producers and media.
- Secondary research requires not just basic information literacy but also philosophical and epistemological perspectives (thinking carefully about what kinds of knowledge you want to produce, and where your scholarly authority is going to come from), psychological resources (staying rational and motivated) and organizational skill (efficient time management).

References

Abram, Simone. 2003. 'Anthropologies in Policies, Anthropologies in Places: Reflections on Fieldwork "in" Documents and Policies.' In T. H. Eriksen (ed.), *Globalization: Studies in Anthropology*. London: Pluto Press, pp. 138–57.

Atkinson, Paul and Martyn Hammersley. 2007. *Ethnography: Principles in Practice*. 3rd edition. London: Routledge.

Benedict, Ruth. 1989 (1946). *The Chrysanthemum and the Sword*. 2nd edition. Boston, MA: Houghton Mifflin.

Booth, Andrew. 2001. 'Cochrane or Cock-eyed? How Should We Conduct Systematic Reviews of Qualitative Research?' http://www.leeds.ac.uk/educol/documents/00001724.htm (accessed 30 November 2012).

Brettell, Caroline. 1998. 'Fieldwork in the Archives: Methods and Sources in Historical Anthropology'. In H. R. Bernard (ed.), *Handbook of Methods in Cultural Anthropology*. Walnut Creek, CA: AltaMira Press, pp. 513–46.

Britten, Nicky and Catherine Pope. 2012. 'Medicine Taking for Asthma: A Worked Example of Meta-ethnography'. In K. Hannes and C. Lockwood (eds), *Synthesizing Qualitative Research: Choosing the Right Approach*. London: Wiley-Blackwell, pp. 41–58.

De Munck, Victor. 2009. *Research Design and Methods for Studying Cultures*. Lanham, MD: AltaMira.

Doyle, Lynn H. 2003. 'Synthesis Through Meta-ethnography: Paradoxes, Enhancements, and Possibilities', *Qualitative Research*, 3(3): 321–44.

Glaser, Barney and Anselm Strauss. 1967. *The Discovery of Grounded Theory: Strategies for Qualitative Research*. New York: Aldine and Atherton.

Hewson, Claire, Peter Yule, Dianna Laurent and Carl Vogel. 2003. *Internet Research Methods: A Practical Guide for the Social and Behavioural Sciences*. London: Sage.

Imel, Susan. 2011. 'Writing a Literature Review'. In T. S. Rocco and T. Hatcher (eds), *The Handbook of Scholarly Writing and Publishing*. San Francisco: Jossey-Bass, pp. 145–60.

Kozinets, R. V. 2010. *Netnography: Doing Ethnographic Research Online*. London: Sage.

Matsutake Worlds Research Group. 2009. 'Strong Collaboration as a Method for Multi-sited Ethnography: On Mycorrhizal Relations'. In M. Falzon (ed.), *Multi-Sited Ethnography*. Farnham, UK: Ashgate, pp. 197–214.

Mauss, Marcel. 1969 (1925). *The Gift: Forms and Functions of Exchange in Archaic Societies* (Trans: Ian Cunnison). London: Cohen and West.

Open University (UK) SAFARI (online student guide to information for research), http://www.open.ac.uk/safari (accessed 30 November 2012).

Pawluch, Dorothy, William Shaffir and Charlene Miall. 2005. *Doing Ethnography: Studying Everyday Life*. Toronto: Canadian Scholars Press.

Sahlins, Marshall. 1972 (1968). 'Notes on the Original Affluent Society', reprinted in M. Sahlins, *Stone Age Economics*. London: Tavistock, pp. 1–39.

TutorPro Virtual Training Suite (online student guide to internet research), http://www.vtstutorials.co.uk (accessed 30 November 2012).

Whitehead, Neil and Michael Wesch (eds). 2012. *Human No More: Digital Subjectivities, Unhuman Subjects, and the End of Anthropology*. Boulder: University of Colorado Press.

4 Doing research
Anthropology and ethnographic fieldwork

Joost Fontein

Before we address the practicalities of doing fieldwork, this chapter takes a more detailed look at the relationship between anthropology and fieldwork methods. Primary ethnographic fieldwork remains something of a sacred cow in anthropology. Venerated as a key 'rite of passage', it is often celebrated as idiosyncratic and something that can only be learnt by doing. While acknowledging the contingency inherent to all fieldwork, this chapter considers the vital relationship that exists between research questions, theoretical or anthropological perspectives and fieldwork methods. Different projects (and different aspects of the same project) often require different methods and approaches, and the main purpose of this chapter is to consider the possibilities offered by a broad range of fieldwork repertoires. Our focus here is on primary fieldwork but many aspects of discussion apply equally to secondary or library-based research projects.

'Deep hanging out': what is ethnographic fieldwork anyway?

Fieldwork is a 'rite of passage'?

It is something of a disciplinary truism to describe primary ethnographic fieldwork as anthropologists' own 'sacred rite of passage'. Peacock, for example, likens the anthropologist's experience of fieldwork to that of Yurri Zhivago (in the famous novel by Boris Pasternak), fleeing the Russian revolution to the 'radically new situation' of the unfamiliar world of rural Siberia, and notes that fieldwork 'is said to be radically self-transforming', 'like psychoanalysis' or 'brainwashing'; an 'initiation ritual that … moves the initiate to a new level of maturity', like 'one is "born again"' (Peacock 1986: 49–50 and 55). Unfortunately such sentiments are often a precursor to all sorts of mystifications, which can leave researchers doing fieldwork for the first time at a loss as to what they are actually going to do, what they are committing themselves to, and what the point of it all really is. The purpose of this chapter and the next is to cut through these mystifications and to offer practical guidance without turning the liberating and enriching idiosyncrasies of different fieldwork styles, approaches and experiences into something too formulaic and thereby impoverished.

As anthropology students learn early on, one of the earliest champions of ethnographic fieldwork in anthropology was Bronisław Malinowski. He famously urged anthropologists 'off the veranda' to take part in the lives of people they were studying over sustained periods of time and in far greater depth than before, thereby gaining better understandings of their meaningful lives, societies and culture (Young 2004). Prior to this ethnographic awakening, much, if not most anthropology had been done on a secondary basis, from the reports of travellers, missionaries and colonial officials. Since then, fieldwork has become something of a 'rite of passage', often (but falsely) identified exclusively with social or cultural anthropology as a discipline, and frequently taken as marking a young scholar's 'coming of age' as an anthropologist in their own right. Although the classic 'village ethnography' has become something of a rarity – as the world has changed and anthropological questions and concepts have moved on – the continuing importance of an anthropologist's first substantive field project is reflected in the recognition still given to ethnographic mono-graphs in the discipline, and the anecdotal nostalgia with which anthropologists often talk of their first trip into 'the field'. Indeed, any conversation or written account about ethnographic fieldwork (including this one) is often awash with amusing anecdotes and interesting but insubstantial titbits.

This anecdotal tendency repeats itself in the kind of advice that established anthropologists claim they were first given before setting out to try to their hand at fieldwork. Evans-Pritchard once reflected on the fieldwork advice he had been given as a novice himself (1983 [1937]: 239–54, cited in Eriksen 2001: 26). This included instructions not to 'converse with an informant for more than twenty minutes because if you aren't bored by that time he will be', which he commented was 'very good advice if somewhat inadequate'. As field sites have become more diverse and multiple, and informants with ample spare time to converse with researchers much harder to find, this advice probably has stronger resonance today than it did in Evans-Pritchard's time. He was told by another contemporary 'that it was really all quite simple; one should always behave as a gentleman', which today we may interpret in terms of the importance of respect and ethics in 'the field'. His instructor Charles Seligman told him 'to take ten grammes of quinine every night and to keep off women', and Evans-Pritchard advised his own student 'not to be a bloody fool'. While anthropologists often find themselves in the 'role of the clown' and at other times as 'the expert' (Eriksen 2001: 24), today we might equally emphasize the importance of looking after oneself physically, but also socially, emotionally and psychologically. Field-work can be very arduous in different ways. But as Eriksen helpfully notes (2001: 26), in the same account Evans-Pritchard much more usefully empha-sized that 'facts are themselves fairly meaningless', that 'one must know precisely what one wants to know' and then fashion a suitable methodology from available techniques. This *is* useful advice and is something we return to later.

Fieldwork is 'I was there'?

Perhaps more important than the continuing status of the ethnographic monograph in the discipline, or scholars' own nostalgia for their early fieldwork experiences, ethnographic encounters often remain the base line of anthropological authority. Indeed, the nostalgic, anecdotal tendency that anthropologists sometimes indulge in can seem more like instances of self-legitimation or our own kind of 'cultural capital', than useful, practical advice. However, the ethnographic claim that 'I was there' often remains the (unspoken) basis of anthropological authority. A few years ago a colleague was presenting a seminar on their work on death rituals in Indonesia. His account of people conversing with dead relatives, in the belief that they were not dead until they had finished draining them of their fluids, was met with gasps of astonishment. 'Surely this is a metaphor, they did not really believe these corpses were still alive', was the general thrust of the audience members' response. My colleague's final, on the back foot, retort was: 'I was there, for months watching these people talking to corpses as they were drying.' That was the end of the conversation. An anthropological bottom line had been reached.

Fieldwork is primary research?

As we have highlighted in the previous chapter on secondary research, since fieldwork has gained this mysterious and overwhelming status in anthropology the equally important value of secondary research and archival work has often been overlooked, or left unspoken and unconsidered. As with all scholarship, secondary research remains vital to doing anthropological research, and while it is possible to produce brilliant anthropological papers without fieldwork, it is completely impossible to do so without secondary research. As Chapter 1 discussed, some topics are simply better explored through secondary research. Our experience suggests that many students who choose not to do fieldwork benefit hugely from ensuring their studies are feasible and limited in scope. Conversely, students who do fieldwork sometimes struggle to contain the huge quantities of seemingly disparate and diverse data that they have collected, or match it effectively with equally diverse amounts of secondary information.

As the distinction between fieldwork-based and secondary or library-based research projects increasingly disintegrates (because all anthropological research relies on secondary research, whether or not it is also based on fieldwork), so too does the distinction between primary and secondary data, and between fieldwork and archival or library research. This is because there has been an increasing recognition that an 'ethnographic perspective' can be applied to almost any kind of research. So, as the Comaroffs (1992) have championed, anthropologists (and historians and others) are now often doing 'ethnography in the archives', just as those 'in the field' often spend huge amounts of time collecting, analysing and later writing about, visual and written materials encountered during their fieldwork. Such materials may be anything from newspapers to unpublished reports, letters, notes, official documents, ID forms, licenses and other bureaucratic paperwork, even images and graffiti, through which so much cultural and political life everywhere takes place. Ethnographic fieldwork is perhaps as much an attitude, or way of reading, seeing and being, as it is a bundle of research methods. In this respect, this chapter may be as useful for students not doing 'fieldwork' per se, as it is for those going into 'the field'.

Fieldwork as a diversity of tools and techniques

Ethnographic fieldwork can now take so many forms it has become harder than ever to define it. There are some key methods, concepts or distinctions that are of central importance, such as participant observation, interviews, visual techniques, and other social science methods such as survey work. Most people agree that attention to, and competence in language remains a central concern. Many anthropologists also agree that 'making the familiar strange, and the strange familiar' is key to the ethnographic and anthropological imperative (see Chapter 1). This not only highlights the comparative dimension which remains at the heart of anthropology (however subtle and unacknowledged), but it also dissolves any lingering notion that 'proper anthropology' must be done 'away', in exotic, preferably sun-soaked places.

Despite these shared notions, however, an ethnographer's tool bag is often filled with a diverse but ill-defined array of equipment. Fieldworkers usually pick, mix and refine a variety of research tools to suit their research questions and requirements. Exactly what is participant observation actually? Is it what I am doing just by being there, or do I need to get my hands dirty? How much to observe and how much to participate? Is this conversation included? Or is this an interview? And if so what kind of interview? These are all questions that could preoccupy us for a long time and most ethnographers will face them at some moment during their fieldwork. As with all qualitative kinds of research, spending too much time trying to define what exactly it is that we are doing may be counter-productive. At the same time, however, we should always reflect upon what we are doing and why, because it is in this way that our fieldwork methods, or tools, become sharpened according to the needs of a particular project. This is also one reason why fieldwork takes time and why different projects, and different periods of the same project, often demand different kinds of toolkits.

Surveys and quantitative work are a different kettle of fish in this regard perhaps, and indeed this is why they are often attractive; their systematic nature and that of the data they generate, appears to give them an aura of authority, as stable bases upon which to build our rich, but idiosyncratic and often unrepeatable ethnographic collections of events, actions, utterances and experiences. But, as we warned in Chapter 3, quantitative data must also be subject to reflection, evaluation and if necessary, critique.

Fieldwork is 'deep hanging out'?

For all these reasons and more, fieldwork remains something of a mystery and any definition seems elusive. Sometimes, anthropological fieldwork is compared, favourably or otherwise, with travel writing (Peacock 1986: 49–54), but although some great anthropological classics, such as Lévi-Strauss's *Tristes*

Tropiques (1976 [1955]), have taken a similar form, the two are fundamentally differentiated by intent and purpose, by the specific questions the anthropological fieldworker is seeking to ask and resolve, and by the importance of thorough, systematic empirical recording of events, experiences and exchanges. One preferred short, if facetious, definition is 'deep hanging out', because on the surface of it, this is what it appears anthropologists are doing with so much of their time 'in the field'. But of course this is itself not particularly useful. Fieldwork can be arduous, exhausting and anxiety-provoking, as well as fun, inspiring and hugely rewarding. It takes time, and while few anthropologists these days spend years in the field as they once did, they are still often doing fieldwork for what seems like unusually long periods of time, particularly when compared to other social scientists doing statistical research or questionnaire surveys, or 'development' consultants using rapid or participatory rural appraisal techniques (see Box 5.1 in the next chapter). Of course, anthropology students writing dissertations will usually be doing fieldwork for much shorter periods – only a few weeks or maybe months at the very most – so one of the challenges you will face will be making the most of a limited timeframe. Even if 'deep hanging out' is what you are doing most of the time, this will involve other fieldwork methods and many hours of writing notes, meaning that the daily routines of fieldwork can be much more demanding than the notion of 'deep hanging out' implies. More importantly, 'deep hanging out', while reflecting superficially what we may appear to be doing 'in the field', does not effectively capture what we think we are doing, and more importantly, *why* we are doing it. This brings us back once again to Evans-Pritchard's point about 'knowing what one wants to know' and the question 'what is anthropology about anyway?' which we discussed in Chapter 1. If thinking about what anthropology is and how we understand it is crucial for coming up with research projects and specific research questions, it is also by extension key to thinking about and doing fieldwork. We return to this critical point later.

A useful fieldwork definition

For the moment though, let us satisfy ourselves with a definition of 'ethnographic fieldwork' provided by Willis and Trondman (2000: 5). Ethnography, they say:

> Is a family of methods involving direct and sustained social contact with agents, and of richly writing up the encounter, respecting, recording, representing at least partly *in its own terms*, the irreducibility of human experience. Ethnography is the deliberate witness-cum-recording of human events.

In many respects, this is a useful definition with which to proceed. It acknowledges that a variety of methods are involved in fieldwork, but stresses that they all involve 'direct and sustained social contact'. This social dimension is key to all fieldwork, even if the 'agents' involved, are not necessarily people, as some recent trends in anthropological theory might seek to stress. If, for example, you decide to adopt a 'follow the object' approach, perhaps in the style of Appadurai's the 'social life of things' (1986), then you could consider that the key 'agent' is the thing, commodity or artifact around which your study is centred, but the chances are you would still be generating your data through social contact with others around you. This equally applies if you are following an issue, a 'metaphor', a 'ritual' or whatever. This social dimension illustrates one of the unique aspects of fieldwork, which is the way in which the ethnographer him or herself is the central tool of research. This is also part of what can make fieldwork personally demanding. Willis and Trondman's definition also gives due recognition to the importance of ethics (the references to 'respect' for example), to wholism ('the irreducibility of human experiences'), and importantly, to writing and recording ('the deliberate witness-cum-recording of human events'). The reference to 'richly writing' can be seen as a nod to Geertz's (1973) notion of 'thick description', and implied here too is the importance of interpretation.

Key points

- Fieldwork is learnt by doing, but preparation and self-reflection during the process are the means by which fieldworkers hone their tools to suit their research projects.
- Ethnographic fieldwork can be as much a way of reading, seeing and being, as a defined set of tools.

What is anthropology anyway (part 2), and why does this matter for doing fieldwork?

If thinking about what anthropology is, is crucial both to identifying research projects and formulating more precise research questions once you have begun to build a research project (see Chapters 1 and 2), then it follows that it is also crucial to how you do fieldwork. In this section we take a deeper and more detailed look at different methodological approaches and their relation to different theoretical concerns. Here the question of analytical or theoretical frameworks *does* become important. A comparison between the anthropological or theoretical frameworks of four different anthropologists, and how this was reflected in their fieldwork and writing, may be a useful illustration here. Let's take Victor Turner (1964), Kevin Dwyer (1982), Thomas Csordas (1994) and Loïc Wacquant (1995) in turn, in order to explore how theoretical perspectives and anthropological positioning have important implications for our approach to fieldwork, and for how we gather, deal with and interpret data in 'the field'.

Victor Turner's 'Symbols in Ndembu Ritual'

As anthropology students will recognize, Victor Turner was interested in symbols, their meanings, and their role in social processes. In his words:

> For symbols are essentially involved in social process. I came to see performances of ritual as distinct phases in the social processes whereby groups became adjusted to internal changes and adapted to their external environment. From this standpoint the ritual symbol becomes a factor in social action, a positive force in an activity-field. The symbol becomes associated with human interests, purposes, ends and means, whether these are explicitly formulated or have to be inferred from the observed behaviour. The structure and purposes of a symbol become those of a dynamic entity, at least within its appropriate context of action.
>
> (Turner 1964: 21)

In his famous 'Symbols in Ndembu Ritual' (1964) he uses an analysis of the *Nkang'a*, a girls' puberty ritual, of the Ndembu of Zambia, to illustrate how symbols do things, and importantly for our purposes, what the methodological implications are for ethnographers studying 'ritual symbols'. Crucial to Turner's approach was the belief that 'it was methodologically important to keep observational and interpretive material distinct from one another' (ibid.: 20). More importantly, Turner also emphasized the separation of the 'emic' (although he did not use this phrase) interpretations of informants, from the 'etic' interpretations of the ethnographer. So Turner's approach involved a separation of 'three classes of data' (ibid.: 21):

- External form and observable characteristics.
- Interpretations offered:
  i) by specialists
  ii) by laymen
- Significant contexts largely worked out by the anthropologist.

From a very practical point of view, we can see that each of these 'classes of data' requires different kinds of fieldwork techniques and practices. First, the external form and observable characteristics are best acquired through participant observation in the rituals. Second, 'local' interpretations are best elicited through extensive conversations and interviews with informants. Third, Turner's 'significant contexts' may be worked out through both participant observation in/of, and interviews about, the events themselves, but also before, after and more generally in Ndembu society, as well as much broader data gathering, including 'secondary' research of various kinds.

What Turner does very convincingly in 'Symbols in Ndembu Ritual' is show how crucial symbols in this ritual – in particular what he calls 'the milk-tree' (the *mudyi* tree or *Diplorrhyncus mossambicensis*) – take on a layering of different meanings for different Ndembu informants and the 'outside' ethnographer, which relate at once to its physical characteristics and the internal workings of Ndembu social structure. For example, the 'milky beads' of latex that the tree exudes, link to the tree's role as a symbolic representation of 'human breast milk'; the 'nurturance between mother and child'; the domestic social ties breast feeding implies; and therefore matriliny, 'the principle upon which the continuity of Ndembu society depends'. Furthermore, Turner shows how 'important symbols may themselves be symbols', and thereby suggests that for ritual specialists in particular, the milk-tree comes to symbolize 'the total system of inter-relations between groups and persons' of Ndembu society, so that 'at its highest level of abstraction … the milk-tree stands for the unity and continuity of Ndembu society' (1964: 21).

Moving beyond 'emic' interpretations, Turner argues that 'when the third mode of interpretation, contextual analysis, is applied':

> The interpretations of informants are contradicted by the way people actually behave with reference to the milk-tree. It becomes clear that the milk-tree represents aspects of social differentiation, and even opposition between the components of a society which ideally it is supposed to symbolize as a harmonious whole.
>
> (Turner 1964: 24)

He then goes on to discuss a series of social distinctions, discriminations and oppositions (between men and women; between the initiate and 'the moral community of adult women'; between the 'matricentric family' and wider society; between virilocality and matriliny; and between matrilineage groups and the totality of society made up of such groups) which the milk-tree, and the *Nkang'a* ritual in which it has such a key position, represents and reinforces. For Turner then, symbols can operate beyond the awareness of ritual participants. The important theoretical and methodological point here is that the interpretation of the ethnographer cannot simply be acquired by gathering the 'emic' interpretations of different informants. It requires more, and as Turner himself discusses, a crucial question then becomes 'meaning for whom?' (1964: 27).

Turner deliberately positions his perspective against those of other contemporary anthropologists of his time, for example, Nadel, for whom: 'uncomprehended symbols have no part in social enquiry; their effectiveness lies in their capacity to indicate, and if they indicate nothing to the actors, they are, from our point of view, irrelevant, and indeed no longer symbols' (Nadel 1954: 108, cited in Turner 1964: 27).

He also criticises Monica Wilson's emphasis on Nyakyusa interpretations of their own rituals and denigration of anthropologists' 'symbolic guessing' and 'the ethnographer's interpretations of the rituals of other people' (Wilson 1957: 6, cited in Turner 1964: 28), arguing that 'these investigators go beyond the limits of salutary caution and impose serious, and even arbitrary, limitations upon themselves'. Such perspectives or approaches, Turner argues 'must ignore or regard as irrelevant some of the crucial properties of such symbols' (1964: 28). The theoretical substance of this debate is not our primary concern here, rather, the point is that Turner's theoretical perspective and his anthropological positioning on the nature and social efficacy of ritual symbols had important implications for his approach to fieldwork; how he conducted research and interpreted data in 'the field'.

Some years later, following anthropology's crisis of representation during the 1980s and in the face of powerful post-structuralist and postcolonial critique of the status of anthropological knowledge, a new phase in ethnographic field-work emerged. Coming particularly in the wake of Clifford and Marcus's (1986) *Writing Culture*, and growing recognition that anthropology needed to be more reflexive about its own methods, a series of new experimental eth-nographies sought to limit the imposition or mediation of the ethnographer's own interpretations in favour of new kinds of cooperative, inter-subjective, deductive accounts of ethnographic encounters, in which anthropologists attempted shared authorship with their informants. You may wish to consult Spencer's (1989) useful discussion and critique of these approaches (see also Beal 1995), but for our purposes here let us consider Kevin Dwyer's (1982) *Moroccan Dialogues*, which in many respects is paradigmatic of this phase in anthropology's relationship to fieldwork. Again, our principle concern is less the broader anthropological debates themselves than to illustrate how different fieldwork approaches are intimately linked to how we see and understand anthropology, in order to help you think about the kind of fieldwork your project might require, or be enriched by.

Kevin Dwyer's Moroccan Dialogues

Dwyer states that when he went to Morocco to do fieldwork in 1975 he deliberately did so 'with no specific research task planned' (1982: 21). This was against the current of most anthropology at the time, and is to some extent against our advice that you should have a clear idea what you are seeking to do before you begin. Dwyer's approach was driven by his suspicion that:

> a clear research project, designed to respond to current theoretical concerns in anthropology, would tend to suppress and severely distort the sponta-neity and normal behaviour of people I encountered, forcing them to fit categories, modes and aspects defined by the project.
>
> (Dwyer 1982: 21)

Of course we can see that in fact Dwyer did have a purpose: to explore new forms of ethnographic representation, which might allow his informant's views and understanding of the world to come across more directly, unhindered by the ethnographer's own interpretative intervention. In a sense his ethnographic approach was an explicitly 'collaborative' one, in which the end product is a result of an amalgamation of the different interests of the fieldworker and informant, forged in (more or less) equal, conversational contexts. Of course, in many respects all fieldwork is collaborative in this way, and perhaps what sets Dwyer's work apart is his explicit effort to reduce the weight of the ethnographer's imprint. His book amounts to a series of transcribed (taped) conversations and unstructured interviews with a single informant, Faqir Muhammad, whom he had come to know very well during previous research visits to Morocco. Dwyer states early on that he was trying to explore 'what was the relationship between the Faqir, a Moroccan villager, and me, a New Yorker built upon?' (1982: 22). Furthermore 'what significance did this relationship have for the practice of anthropology?' He felt, perhaps correctly, that although anthropology 'takes the encounter between individuals of different societies as its primary research tool ... this relationship had had no explicit place in the genres other anthropologists had written in'. 'Finally' he states that he 'was dismayed that, with so much of my relationship with the Faqir expressed verbally, my written notes captured it so inadequately and most of it was quickly lost as my memory of it faded' (1982: 21).

The purpose of Dwyer's research was to examine the nature of ethnographic fieldwork, to explore the ethnographer's relationships with informants created in the very context of fieldwork, and to experiment with new forms of recording and representation which would allow the inter-subjective nature of these relationships to be better captured and communicated. The extent to which he, or any researcher or writer for that matter, could actually achieve this in research and a book that they have ultimately authored themselves remains debatable, and this is something that Spencer (1989) also comments on.

Nevertheless, it is clear that Dwyer's anthropological quest defined not only his writing but also the manner in which he did his fieldwork. Compared with Turner, for whom the 'emic' interpretations of informants and the 'etic' interpretations of the anthropologist are distinct (and this distinction is of great significance for the anthropological project of understanding what and how symbols do things), for Dwyer this distinction deliberately falls away or is collapsed in the explicit project of trying to avoid what had come to be seen as the 'violence' of anthropological representation. In this project both 'the external form and observable characteristics' and the 'significant contexts largely worked out by the anthropologist', as Turner put it, are put on the back burner in favour of the 'interpretations' or meanings offered by the informants themselves. And this is clearly reflected in the fieldwork approaches adopted. So for Dwyer's *Moroccan Dialogues*, it is taped, informal conversations and unstructured interviews that form the key fieldwork method. Participant observation, broader contextual data gathering, and secondary research, are relegated to the backstage, and more 'formal' techniques such as focus group discussions, surveys and questionnaires, do not appear at all. Of course, arguments could be made about the continuing significance of secondary reading, participant observation and broader data gathering in Dwyer's fieldwork – for example, in informing the kinds of questions Dwyer asked the Faqir during their interviews and conversations – nevertheless, for our purposes, here is a second clear example of

how the anthropological questions a project is concerned with affect the fieldwork methods deployed.

Underpinning Dwyer's 'experimental' fieldwork and ethnography, and
others like it which sought to let the 'subaltern speak' (paraphrasing Spivak
1988), is an assumption that the conscious or 'mindful' meaning and knowledge of informants is key to the anthropological project.[1] This assumption
and anthropological positioning in part determined the nature of their ethnographic fieldwork. This anthropological assumption came under increasing
scrutiny in subsequent years with growing anthropological interest in questions
of 'embodiment' and 'practice'. Of course, these new theoretical turns also
made their own particular fieldwork demands. To illustrate this let's turn to
Thomas Csordas's 1994 chapter in his edited collection *Embodiment and
Experience*, and Loïc Wacquant's equally seminal article 'The Pugilistic Point of
View' (1995). In both cases we can see how their anthropological thinking
was influenced by phenomenology and particularly by the work of Pierre
Bourdieu.

Csordas's 'Words from the Holy People: A Case Study in Cultural Phenomenology' and Wacquant's 'The Pugilistic Point of View'

For Csordas, 'embodiment' is 'a methodological standpoint in which bodily
experience is understood to be the existential ground of culture and self' (1994:
269). His research explored the 'experiential understanding of being-in-the-
world' of a young Navajo man afflicted with brain cancer. Because his 'cultural
phenomenology' was determined to understand 'both biology and culture' as
'forms of objectification or representation', one of his crucial goals was 'to
show how cultural meaning is intrinsic to embodied experience on the existential level of being-in-the world' (1994: 270). This already implies that the
interview- and conversation-heavy process that was a central feature of Dwyer's
work would not be sufficient, and indeed, Csordas's fieldwork was based both
on conversations and observation over a period of two years. However, Csordas's phenomenological conviction that 'cultural meaning is intrinsic to embodied experience' also denies Turner's penchant for 'significant contexts worked
out by the anthropologist'. If, as Csordas argues (following Merleau-Ponty
1962), we carry the social 'inseparably with us before any objectification'
(1994: 270), then the status of 'social facts' or 'significant contexts' changes
profoundly. These do not pre-exist before or external to our embodied
experience in the world – ready for the anthropologist's interpretation – but
are exactly, as he says, 'intrinsic to them'. This has important ramifications for
his fieldwork. In recognizing that both 'biology' and 'culture' – 'neuropathol-
ogy' and religion in this case – are forms of objectifying an experience, Csordas
argues that neither alone are sufficient for understanding the cancer patient's
experience or its meaning for him. Rather, what Csordas does in his account is
to 'thread the discussion of being-in-the-world between the two poles of
objectification' in order to show how his informant 'brought to bear the

symbolic resources of his culture to create meaning for a life plunged into profound existential crisis, and to formulate a life plan consistent with his experience of chronic neurological disease' (1994: 270). On the surface, Csordas employs very similar ethnographic methods or tools as Turner, but the ethnographic approach, attitude or positioning is profoundly different. Consequently, the kind of fieldwork this type of project demands, and the kind of fieldnotes and other 'raw' data it produces are likely to be substantially different.

Working within a broadly similar kind of anthropological framework, Loïc Wacquant's 'The Pugilistic Point of View' took the importance of experience, practice, situational being-in-the-world, and therefore of 'participant observation' in fieldwork, to a different level. Emphasizing that his approach was 'emphatically not ... premised simply on an empathetic "thick description" of the lived experience of prizefighting' or 'an interpretive dissection of "the native's point of view"' (1995: 490), because it is questionable whether a *single* 'native point of view' ever exists, or 'whether the so-called native may be said to have a "point of view" at all, rather than *being one with* the universe of which he partakes' (1995: 490–1), Wacquant spent three years training to be a boxer and (deep) 'hanging out' with boxers in Chicago. In many ways this was 'observant-participation' rather than participant observation. It was only in the third year that he carried out in-depth, semi-structured interviews with 50 boxers.

This long immersion enabled Wacquant not only to acquire 'the half-articulate, quasi organic belief in the value of the game and its stakes, inscribed deep within the body through progressive incorporation of its core tenets' (1995: 492–3) – the habitus of boxing we might say – but also to build 'solid friendships' of 'trust and mutual respect' which enriched his subsequent interviews. It meant, in his words, that he was 'able to phrase my questions in a manner congruent with their occupational concerns and thus elicit candid and meaningful answers, which I could also confront with extensive direct observation and check against related accounts by strategically situated informants' (1995: 493). Furthermore, unlike the question mark that Csordas raises about the status of 'social facts' (and in tune with Bourdieu's (1992) own account of the importance of 'reflexivity' as a means of making scholarship more 'objective'), Wacquant also used the time that he was training to conduct more conventional research on 'the social structures of marginality in Chicago's inner city' (1995: 493).

This combination of deep immersion, 'observant participation' and 'learning the craft', alongside substantial interviews and broader research into the 'significant contexts' of boxing in Chicago, enabled Wacquant to produce an unrivalled and much cited ethnographic account. In his view, it was inevitably 'a *(re)construction* of the "pugilistic point of view", that is the synthetic view of professional boxing one can gain from the various points that may be occupied within the structure of social and symbolic relations that make up the pugilistic field' (1994: 491). Yet few would contend that Wacquant's article is one of sociology and anthropology's most widely celebrated, recent ethnographic accounts. For our purposes here, it illustrates brilliantly how the nature of any fieldwork experience and approach is determined both by the specific research questions and the broader theoretical frameworks deriving from the anthropological assumptions embedded within the research design, and therefore how the selection of research methods, or tools, is unique for every project. At the same time it shows how any ethnographic fieldwork is necessarily centred on and around the person and body of the researcher themselves. Indeed, in many respects Wacquant is useful here because his fieldwork most clearly shared aspects, techniques and approaches with all three of the other anthropologists that we have discussed, even as it stands out as markedly different from any one of them.

Of course, many of the aspects of fieldwork deployed by these different authors will be beyond the time limits of your own anthropology project. It is unlikely you will have the opportunity to spend three years learning to box, or to acquire a 'pugilistic habitus' if you prefer. Interviewing and observing cancer patients for almost two years would probably defy not only the time available to you, but also any ethical review board tasked with considering student research proposals. It is also unlikely you will have the time available to transcribe a lengthy series of biographical interviews, even if you found an interesting informant, or rather one interested enough in you, to do the kind of experimental work that Dwyer championed. But our purpose in discussing these examples is less to offer alternatives for fieldwork, than to illustrate how fieldwork techniques and practices, and the nature of the ethnographic data that your fieldwork will generate, is inherently related to both the larger anthropological frameworks within which your project is located, and the specific questions you are seeking to address. You *will* have to find your own way, and hopefully this will be an enjoyable and enlightening experience. Reading other ethnographic works, scrutinizing the methods they deployed and why, will help in this process and encourage you to be reflexive about your own fieldwork.

Key points

- Anthropological assumptions and perspectives carried within your research project, and within the specific questions you are addressing will, in part, determine how you go about collecting field data. It is important to reflect on this before and during your fieldwork.
- Read other ethnographies as you are designing your project and think about the relationship between different kinds of anthropology and the fieldwork tools they imply or require.
- Think about the kind of, and status of, knowledge you are seeking to gather. Interpretation does not just come after the gathering of information, but is embedded in the very processes and methods by which it is collected, or rather, generated in the field.

As **Janet** is preparing for her research, exploring different methodological approaches other anthropologists have adopted and their relationship to different theoretical concerns, she begins to recognize that her interest in the corporeal aesthetics involved in funerary practices in Mexico might make certain kinds of demands upon her fieldwork. She is particularly interested in phenomenological approaches and begins to think about how she could make use of these in her fieldwork. Inspired by the success of Wacquant's efforts to learn the art of boxing she realizes that she could get a better grasp of the aesthetics involved in undertaking by taking part and learning some of the basic skills involved in embalming processes. She therefore changes her earlier decision not to come in contact with dead bodies and asks her hosts in an email if they would be happy to teach her some of the basics of their trade. In their response her prospective undertaker hosts are very keen to teach her some of the tools and techniques of their trade, and Janet becomes increasingly excited about the rich kind of ethnographic material that could be generated by taking part in her hosts' embalming practices.

As his fieldwork draws near and his reading progresses, **John** begins to recognize that most previous studies of gambling have a tendency to 'pathologize' gambling from the outset. He feels that this is inadequate, and realizes he needs to formulate his fieldwork approach around a stance that is centred on his informants' understanding of their own gambling habits and enjoyments. He is particularly influenced by Dwyer's determination not to impose meaning upon his Moroccan informant, and to experiment with new forms of biographical ethnography. John decides that this is the approach that best suits his anthropological stance, and determines that he too will focus his fieldwork upon lengthy, in-depth and repeated, informal and open-ended conversations with a small number of key greyhound owners and gamblers.

References

Appadurai, Arjun (ed.). 1986. *The Social Life of Things: Commodities in Cultural Perspective.* Cambridge: Cambridge University Press.

Beal, Anne M. 1995. 'Reflections on Ethnography in Morocco: A Critical Reading of Three Seminal Texts', *Critique of Anthropology*, 15(3): 289–304.

Bourdieu, Pierre. 1992. 'Participant Objectivation'. In P. Bourdieu and L. Wacquant, *An Invitation to Reflexive Sociology*. Chicago: University of Chicago Press.

Clifford, James and George Marcus. 1986. *Writing Culture: The Poetics and Politics of Ethnography*. Berkeley: University of California Press.

Comaroff, John and Jean Comaroff. 1992. *Ethnography and the Historical Imagination*, Boulder, CO: Westview Press.

Crapanzano, Victor. 1985. *Tuhami: Portrait of a Moroccan*. Chicago: Chicago University Press.

Csordas, Thomas. 1994. 'Words from the Holy People: A Case Study in Cultural Phenomenology'. In T. Csordas (ed.), *Embodiment and Experience: The Existential Ground of Culture and Self*. Cambridge: Cambridge University Press, pp. 269–90.

Dwyer, Kevin. 1982. *Moroccan Dialogues: Anthropology in Question*. Prospect Heights, IL: Waveland Press.

Eriksen, Thomas, H. 2001 (1995). *Small Places, Large Issues: An Introduction to Social and Cultural Anthropology*. 2nd edition. London: Pluto Press.

Evans-Pritchard, E. E. 1983 (1937). *Witchcraft, Magic and Oracles Among the Azande*. Oxford: Oxford University Press.

Geertz, Clifford. 1973. 'Thick Description: Toward an Interpretative Theory of Culture', In Clifford Geertz, *The Interpretation of Cultures*. New York: Basic Books, pp. 3–30.

Lévi-Strauss, Claude. 1976 (1955). *Tristes Tropiques* (Trans. J. Weightman and D. Weightman). Harmondsworth: Penguin.

Merleau-Ponty, Maurice. 1962. *Phenomenology of Perception*. London and New York: Routledge.

Nadel, Siegfried F. 1954. *Nupe Religion*. London: Routledge.

Peacock, James L. 1986. *The Anthropological Lens: Harsh Light, Soft Focus*. Cambridge: Cambridge University Press.

Rabinow, Paul. 1977. *Reflections on Fieldwork in Morocco*. Berkeley: University of California Press.

Spencer, Jonathan. 1989. 'Anthropology as a Kind of Writing', *Man*, 24(1): 145–64.

Spivak, Gayatri S. 1988. 'Can the Subaltern Speak?' In C. Nelson and G. Lawrence (eds), *Marxism and the Interpretation of Culture*. Urbana/Chicago: University of Illinois Press, pp. 271–313.

Turner, Victor. 1964. 'Symbols in Ndembu Ritual'. In M. Gluckman (ed.), *Closed Systems and Open Minds: The Limits of Naivety in Social Science*. Edinburgh: Oliver and Boyd, pp. 20–51.

Wacquant, Loïc. 1995. 'The Pugilistic Point of View: How Boxers Think and Feel about Their Trade', *Theory and Society*, 24(4): 489–535.

Willis, Paul and Mats Trondman. 2000. 'Manifesto for Ethnography', *Ethnography*, 1(1): 5–16.

Wilson, Monica. 1957. *Rituals of Kinship among the Nyakyusa*. London: Oxford University Press.

Young, Michael. 2004. *Malinowski: Odyssey of an Anthropologist 1884–1920*. Yale: Yale University Press.

Note

1 Several of these also focused on Morocco; see, for example, Crapanzano's *Tuhami: Portrait of a Moroccan* (1985), and Rabinow's *Reflections on Fieldwork in Morocco* (1977).

5   Doing research

Fieldwork practicalities

Joost Fontein

This chapter follows from the previous one by focusing on the practicalities of 'doing' ethnographic fieldwork and living in 'the field'. Exploring different fieldwork techniques, it offers practical advice for writing fieldnotes, recording experiences, and transforming rich fieldwork encounters into usable forms of ethnographic data. We also consider other aspects of fieldwork and decisions that you will have to think about and make as you develop your own fieldwork style and approach, and begin to generate your ethnographic material.

Arrival in 'the field'

You have finished your preparations. Your research design has been carefully refined, and you know (or think you know) what your research is about, and what your specific research questions are. You have been granted clearance by your ethics board. You have organized visas, permits and permissions, and have got leave of absence from your employment and/or university. You have had your injections, said goodbye to your supervisor, friends and family. You have got on the plane, train, or left your flat. You arrive at your field site. What do you do now?

Where and how to live

This depends upon the nature of your 'field site'. As we discussed in the chapters on getting started and planning a research project, 'field sites' vary tremendously; from a discrete location (be it a village, neighbourhood, or an institution) to a process, ritual, object, issue or even a metaphor. Unless you are doing fieldwork in your hometown (and are therefore staying put), you will need somewhere to live, and this has important implications for how you will go about generating ethnographic data. You should already have made preparations for access to your field site and thought about where you are going to live, although often such arrangements are only finalized once you arrive in the field. There may even be some advantage to not finalizing such details until you have got a sense of what your field site is like on the ground. Researchers who have visited their field site before will have an advantage in this respect. Whatever your situation, it is important to think about the nature of your project, what information you are seeking to gather, and what your fieldwork will involve on a day-to-day level.

There was a (perhaps mythical) time in anthropology when living with informants in the field was perceived as an essential part of ethnographic fieldwork. Certainly, there might be advantages to living directly within your field site: you don't need to go anywhere to do participant observation as it is happening all around you, and you will encounter conversations, utterances and actions that 'day visits' would miss. If you are in the field for a longer period and improving your familiarity with another language, living with informants in their homes will doubtlessly assist you. But there are also disadvantages. Such fieldwork really is fully immersive. You may have little time to yourself, or for writing fieldnotes (a point we return to later). It can be emotionally demanding, especially if you are used to very particular living arrangements, or value your personal space, and of course it is also demanding upon your hosts. More to the point, it may not help you gather the kind of data your project demands. If, for example, you are interested in kinship patterns in downtown Glasgow, living with Glaswegians in their homes might be very significant. Similarly, if you are interested in how rural chiefs in Zimbabwe perform their authority, living at their homestead might be a good way to witness this. Or, if you are interested in how a particular NGO operates, living within an NGO compound might give you access to crucial 'backstage' processes, conversations and events. But if you are interested in, say, sperm donation, where anonymity is often a key concern, living in a sperm donor's home would not generate the information you require, and would likely be an unwelcome imposition. Similarly, if like Alexander Edmonds, you are interested in beauty and plastic surgery, then where you live may be much less significant than the places you visit and do your 'deep hanging out' (see Chapter 1). Even for Loïc Wacquant, one of the most 'immersed fieldworkers' of recent times, where he lived was less important than what he did and where he went on a day-to-day basis (see Chapter 4).

The question of *where*, and *how* to live, should also be considered with practical concerns in mind. You will spend many hours writing fieldnotes, so whether you live with informants in their homes, or choose to live by yourself, you need to build time and space for writing into your daily routine. This may have logistical demands. It is very difficult to write fieldnotes with children peering over your shoulder, for example. You may need a desk and electricity if you are using a computer. You may have transport requirements. There are also your personal habits and health requirements to consider, from food preferences or allergies, to your more obscure wants and needs. Remember there are no brownie points for suffering, and although generating rich and unique data may involve hardships of all sorts, hardship in itself does not necessarily generate good data. You will need to do more than survive your fieldwork to write a good dissertation.

You should also think about the effects your presence will have on your hosts and informants, whether you live with them or not. Aside from the rather naive assumption that one should avoid affecting one's field site for fear of 'contaminating your data' – in many respects an inevitable part of qualitative research – there are important and usually obvious ethical considerations, social obligations and personal niceties to be observed. If there are significant social and financial inequalities between you and your hosts/informants, you must think carefully about how you can suitably 'pay-your-way'. At the same time bear in mind that others' expectations of your financial situation, or your general influence with authorities, for example, may be as grossly distorted from how you understand your own situation, as your initial assumptions about your informants' lives will often be.

Indeed, managing expectations, your own and of others, is a tricky and often under-discussed dimension of doing 'deep hanging out'. Avoid making promises you cannot keep. It should go without saying that all fieldworkers should avoid putting themselves or their informants/hosts in any potential danger, whether simply by their presence or through their research activities. Normally such potentialities will be flagged at the proposal stage, and if there were a possibility of this the project would not have passed ethical review. However, there are often more subtle social dynamics going on, involving much less dramatic or immediate physical or social risks, which field researchers must remain alert and sensitive to. In some contexts, for example, the presence of a foreign researcher living at one household in a village may generate social problems for your hosts, which you or they had not anticipated. This may change during fieldwork, so remain sensitive to your hosts' concerns (they are much more likely to be attuned to this than you are), and you should probably have alternative arrangements planned or considered beforehand, if necessary. Indeed, if you are going to be 'fully immersed' and living for extended periods within a community, it is a good idea to have another place to go and stay, to 'get away' to when you or your hosts need a break.

Plan B

This need for an 'alternative option', or 'Plan B', also applies to your project as a whole. It is not unusual for a carefully refined research plan to suddenly become irrelevant, or un-researchable upon arrival 'in the field', or later on during fieldwork. Circumstances can change, assumptions built into a project may be shown to be without basis, or something much more interesting might be going on which you had not previously been aware of. Researchers doing fieldwork should allow for this 'resistance of the real', otherwise there would be little point doing fieldwork at all. A good example is Jean Briggs's classic Inuit ethnography *Never in Anger* (1970). Briggs set out to study pre-Christian beliefs and practices among the Utku, but then found no one willing to talk about this because they were ashamed of their pre-Christian past. Her rich ethnographic account, describing one of the most arduous kinds of classic fieldwork imaginable, turns on an encounter in which she became very angry with outside traders who damaged an Utku canoe. Her emotional reaction breached a strong social taboo and as a result she was socially ostracized for five months. This is hardly an attractive prospect under any circumstances but certainly not in a severe Arctic context where Briggs was dependent upon her Utku hosts for her every need! Nevertheless, this unfortunate incident revealed a central dynamic of Utku social life to Briggs: the importance of self-restraint and of controlling emotions in one's dealings with others. She subsequently structured her ethnographic account around this hugely significant aspect of Utku life.

It is unlikely that you will be doing fieldwork in quite so arduous or remote a context, nor are you necessarily going to find your research agenda so profoundly challenged. Nevertheless, you should be alert to changing circumstances and factors beyond your own knowledge and control. Allow for contingencies, be prepared to change direction if necessary, and to some extent plan ahead for this. This is not necessarily something to be resisted, but rather welcomed. Sometimes, planning for such contingencies is possible and useful, but not always. It is obviously preferable for any profound changes to take place early on during fieldwork when there is enough time to change direction, focus and methods. This is particularly important if you have committed time and resources into going abroad. You should have a 'Plan B' ready, that you can switch to in the same country or location where you have developed your initial project.

Given the inevitable time constraints of doing ethnographic research, particularly for student researchers, it is advisable to think ahead about possible alternatives, and to spend the first few days or weeks of fieldwork reassessing the feasibility of your project while there is still time to make any changes that realities on the ground require. These kinds of issues may also re-emerge in surprising ways much further into your fieldwork. Be ready to expect, deal with and perhaps embrace, the unexpected.

Key points

- Think about how where (and how) you live will impact your research and the data you generate.
- Balance your research and personal needs with the possible impact of your presence on the lives of your hosts and informants.
- Suffering alone does not necessarily produce good data or dissertations, but be aware that fieldwork can be arduous. Have somewhere to go for 'rest and relaxation', both for you and your hosts.
- Expect the unexpected, allow for the 'resistance of the real', and have a 'Plan B' prepared.

When **Janet** arrives in the Mexican town where her undertaking hosts run their small family business, she is alarmed to discover that the situation is not at all what she had imagined, and that there have been some sudden changes in circumstances. The chief undertaker has died suddenly, leaving his sons in charge of the faltering business. Furthermore, in the context of wider social unrest and proliferating drug-related gang violence, a new Pentecostal move-ment has spread like wildfire across the town. One very significant off-shoot of this social turbulence has been the emergence of new vernacular embalm-ing entrepreneurs, offering new, much more invasive kinds of embalming practices in line with the corporeal demands and religious beliefs of the spreading Pentecostal movement. These have resulted in a dramatic drop in business for Janet's undertaking hosts. The late chief undertaker's son agrees that Janet can still take part in what funerary business they still have coming their way, but this has been drastically reduced to only one or two days of work a week. Janet has to make some quick decisions. She agrees she will attend the funeral parlour to learn embalming techniques for one day a week, but also realizes that she is in a unique position to do research on the rising popularity of the new vernacular embalming entrepreneurs. Keeping one foot lodged in her earlier plan to explore the aesthetics of funerary embalming practices through learning to embalm, she decides to spend the rest of her time seeking out, interviewing and perhaps working with some of these new entrepreneurs. She begins to try to find these vernacular embalming entre-preneurs she has been hearing so much about.

John has been doing fieldwork at the greyhound-racing track for a couple of weeks, in between his part-time job and living at home. He is worried his visits are too brief to build up good rapport with a group of greyhound kennel owners and gamblers who seem to dominate the scene. One day he has a breakthrough. One particularly (if perhaps overly) friendly kennel owner offers him the opportunity of a part-time job at his kennels and a rent-free place to stay at the site. John jumps at this opportunity, and readily gives up his boring part-time job to work four days a week at the kennels, where he has been given a small flat to live in. John is particularly excited because now that he is 'in the field' all the time, he is beginning to collect huge amounts of rich data, and he regularly spends four or five hours an evening writing fieldnotes, between slightly irritating visits to his flat from his new 'landlord/employer/ informant'. He is able to gather more detailed material relating to the human–animal relations of kennel owners, gamblers and greyhounds, and this helps him to build a much thicker understanding of how notions of luck are inter-twined in these emergent relationships.

Generating information

You have been in the field for a week or two. You have found somewhere to live, and your project appears doable. You have begun to seek out informants to talk to, locations and events to attend, observe and participate in. Now it's time to start generating data.

As we have already discussed, although ethnographic fieldwork is hard to define, and different projects require different combinations of styles and approaches, there are several broad research tools which form part of most primary fieldwork repertoires: participant observation, interviews, visual meth-ods, secondary research of all sorts, and to a lesser extent, other social scientific methods such as surveys/questionnaires. Different methods generate different kinds of information and are usually combined in order to address a range of issues, but also to make specific information meaningful in a broader context. It is important to consider methods and their implications before and *during* your research. A key question is: what is it you are trying to find out? Is it about behaviour and relationships or about beliefs, thoughts and ideas, for example? Such questions should determine your methods. Much literature exists with extensive detail of different techniques these methods might involve, and our purpose is not to replicate this here. We do suggest that alongside reading other ethnographies you consult this wider literature for more specific information and to spark your own imagination as to the variety of techniques one can use, as you develop your particular fieldwork style (see Chapter 2 and the companion website for lots of examples). In this chapter we focus on the advantages and disadvantages of three methods most primary fieldwork projects will use: participant observation, interviews and surveys/questionnaires, including the kinds of information these tend to generate.

Participant observation

Participant observation is the quintessential ethnographic fieldwork method championed by Malinowski's call for anthropologists to get 'off the veranda' (or the less comfortable notion of 'going native'). It is a qualitative research method through which the fieldworker takes part in, and so observes, what is going on around them, learning through doing and experiencing as much as through watching and listening. It involves, as Goffman put it, 'subjecting yourself, your own body and your own personality, and your own social situation, to the set of contingencies that play upon a set of individuals, so that you can physically and ecologically penetrate their circle of response to their social situation, or their work situation, or their ethnic situation' (1989: 125, cited in Emerson et al. 1995: 2). Furthermore, 'it involves being with people to see how they respond to events as they happen and experiencing for oneself these events and the circumstances that give rise to them' (Emerson et al. 1995: 2). Although much participant observation does rely upon visual and verbal data, the emphasis on participation and experience also allows for eliciting other kinds of perceptual and embodied knowledge, as Wacquant's extreme example – to embody the bodily dispositions or 'habitus' of boxers – exemplifies.

There is a central and productive tension contained in the very notion of participant observation (or observant participation in Wacquant's case). One participates in order to observe, so one is never either simply a participant nor simply an observer. In this sense, a fieldworker never really 'goes native'. It is questionable, for example, whether the participant observation that Csordas did ever really meant he was able to gauge his Navajo informant's experience of living with cancer. The imperative of observing means that the participation itself is objectified by the fieldwork, and indeed, this is why reflexivity is an essential component of any fieldwork. In practice, many fieldworkers probably observe more than they participate. Indeed, effective and productive participant observation requires a good level of language skills and comprehension, deep social immersion, and a great deal of time, in equal measure.

One of the oft-cited strengths of this relatively unsystematic fieldwork method is its ability to help the fieldworker see the world through another culture' and understand 'what goes without saying'. Certainly, participant observation helps bring out the kinds of non-verbal clues that are often central to social processes and cultural dynamics, and which other methods might not reveal. In this sense, doing participant observation in familiar situations can be as, if not more, productive as that done in unfamiliar settings. This is because participating in order to observe in situations we are familiar with may help make those situations 'strange', and therefore reveal hidden assumptions, behaviours and habits normally taken for granted. By the same token, participant observation in unfamiliar contexts helps us become familiar with and internalize the assumptions, behaviours and habits that at first glance might appear very strange.

Although few anthropologists might admit to this, it is often through making mistakes, whether accidently or more mischievously on purpose – i.e. in participating badly – that such unspoken (familiar or strange) assumptions, habits and behaviours become observable in the first place. Eriksen calls this playing 'the role of the clown' (2001: 24) and fieldworkers often find themselves in this position, involuntarily or otherwise. The 'mistake' that Briggs made was clearly hugely significant for her research.

It is also through participant observation that questions for subsequent interviews are generated. This is very important. Turner's observations about the importance of the milk-tree in the *Nkang'a* ritual, its physical characteristics, as well as the behaviour of his informants during the rituals, enabled him to formulate the questions he then asked initiates and ritual specialists, even as they also influenced his own 'etic' interpretations of the significance of this ritual for Ndembu society. In the examples we discussed in the previous chapter, it was only Dwyer who seems not to have done participant observation for his *Moroccan Dialogues*, but even then it seems clear that previous participant observation informed the questions he asked the Faqir during their lengthy interviews. However, while participant observation was central to the other ethnographies discussed, it was also not enough on its own. Turner, Csordas and Wacquant all also used interviews of various kinds. In fact, it is hard to imagine a successful ethnography based solely on participant observation, because not all the information that a research project requires is accessible through these kinds of immersive methods. Participant observation alone is not necessarily a very useful tool for understanding what people think or feel about a particular issue. This relates in part to why, as the 'violence' of anthropological representations came under critical scrutiny in the 1980s, new experimental ethnographies seemed to move away from doing participant observation in favour of talking directly with informants.

Participant observation will form part of your repertoire, but it is instructive to consider whether, and how, this method is appropriate for your study. Will your informants want to spend time with you? They may be busy or find you annoying, or it may be that your limited technical skills will actually impede the progress of what they are trying to achieve. One fieldworker researching performances of authority by rural chiefs in Zimbabwe thought that he should 'be a proper anthropologist' and help plough fields at the homestead where he was staying. The dry, hard soil was being turned over using hand-held hoes in anticipation of rains likely to fall that afternoon. Against the humoured protests of his hosts he persisted until, before long, his hands were bleeding. Looking up he realized he was not only delaying progress in a field that really needed to be ploughed before lunch time, he was also embarrassing his hosts in front of curious neighbours who were wondering why this foreigner was being made to plough a field! Clearly, participant observation can be a rich source of information, but there are theoretical, ethical and practical limits to 'going native'. In this case, it is hard to see what data could be gained about rural, chiefly authority through delaying and embarrassing your hosts, but if the research sought to explore how means of production produce particular kinds of bodies, attitudes and dispositions, then ploughing a field may have been a central aspect of fieldwork. Participant observation might also offer opportunities to catch utterances and opinions not expressed in other contexts. In some situations, demonstrating your willingness to work hard and show your inadequacies might be an important way of generating questions for later interviews, but also of 'breaking the ice', lowering social barriers, and opening up access to new informants, encounters and events; just as Wacquant's boxing training gave him access to informants he might otherwise never have interviewed.

Interviews

If participant observation alone is not enough you will probably spend much time doing interviews. Interviews come in all shapes and sizes – from highly formalized, structured and strictly time-limited interviews with individual people, to very casual, unstructured conversations with several people, to the kinds of focus group discussions that development researchers tend to adopt. In practice, there are many shades of grey between these poles. In general, informal interviews will be relatively free-flowing whereas structured interviews will involve specific questions prepared in advance. Our purpose here is not to go through the many techniques a researcher can use, but we do encourage you to consult further reference books as you develop your own repertoire (see Chapter 2 and the companion website for examples).

At its most informal, an interview can appear much like a normal conversation. Often the boundary between interviews and the kind of casual conversations common to participant observation is blurred. Sometimes a chance conversation can turn into something akin to an interview, and as long as everyone involved is aware of what is going on, these kinds of encounters-cum-interviews are to be encouraged (see discussion of informed consent in Chapter 6). Many ethnographers admit that much of their ethnographic data emerges from these kinds of conversations, and they are what 'deep hanging out' is often all about. As a rule of thumb, one way of differentiating between a very informal interview and such chance encounters is that an interview is pre-arranged, whether five minutes or five days beforehand. This highlights one central advantage of interviews over participant observation: because they are pre-arranged, interviews offer the fieldworker much more of an opportunity to direct conversation toward the issues, themes and concerns that are of interest to them. By agreeing to be interviewed or to have a conversation, an interviewee has in effect given a green light to the researcher to steer a conversation towards the kinds of data that they are interested in, and they have agreed to devote a certain amount of time to answering your questions. This does *not* in any way absolve a fieldworker from the normal ethical requirements of research, or the social niceties of conversation. We should always respect an informant's wishes regarding confidentiality and their right not to speak on particular subjects. The onus remains on the researcher to generate a situation whereby informants feel free to communicate freely, on their own terms and to their own limits. Yet because an interview is rarely a chance encounter, it allows researchers to come prepared, whether with a vague notion of what he or she wants to cover, or carrying a highly structured list of questions.

Interviews are a good method for gathering verbal data quickly and fieldworkers will use interviews for different purposes at different moments in their research. Early on, interviews with key informants may be directed to obtaining very basic general information. Later on, interviews can become more focused upon particular questions raised by the research (and by other methods), and may be much more formalized. Later interviews can also be much less formalized, if, for example, once basic social or historical information has been acquired, a researcher is looking for richer, evocative ethnographic material about how informants experience or find meaning in particular social situations. Informal, free-flowing interviews can be very useful for gaining deep information on people's life histories, but are likely to be different from an interview with an official about government policy.

The nature of an interview may also depend upon the accessibility of a particular informant, their social status, and your relationship with them. If, like Dwyer, Csordas or Wacquant, your informant is someone you have known well over a long period, you may be able to hold a series of informal interviews. If you are interviewing someone you will be unlikely to talk to again, a busy civil servant or politician, for example, then that interview is likely to be more structured and involve much more pointed questions. How you organize your interviews and whether you ask very open-ended questions or more directed ones, will depend upon what you are trying to achieve, and the context of your relationship with the interviewee. It is often said that an interviewer should try to avoid asking 'leading questions' – questions that prescribe a particular type of answer, or provoke simple yes/no responses. This is good advice for many situations, but like all good advice it should sometimes be taken with a pinch of salt. It is more important to know what you are looking for. If you want rich meaningful data about how an informant understands, thinks about, is motivated by, or experiences something, it is much better to ask open-ended questions that encourage your informant to say as much as they want, in the way that they want. But if you need to know a specific detail, like who said or did what to whom, when and why, then a more pointed, or leading question might be required.

Much depends upon your informant's specific situation, the broader social, cultural, political and historical context of the interview, and the material being discussed. Sometimes this context will be (and will remain) not only beyond your control, but also beyond your knowledge and awareness. There are many 'unknown unknowns' in fieldwork. There are usually many factors which you may never be aware of, and which will determine how 'good' the interview is, how responsive your interviewee, and the kinds of answers you elicit. Be sensitive to the possibility that your informant is under pressures that you might not be aware of, and avoid putting them in uncomfortable or unretrievable positions with your questions. The formality of some kinds of interviews can often hamper natural conversation, however, sometimes informants themselves insist upon a level of formality that the interviewer might find surprising or difficult. Much also depends on your informant's personality traits, mood and motivations. 'Perfect informants', interviewed in 'perfect settings' and with 'perfect' techniques (if such a possibility even exists!) can still lead to poor, uncommunicative interviews. All researchers will be familiar with the frustration of interviews that just 'did not really work'. They are part of the process, and fieldworkers are advised to reflect upon the manner, form and progress of particular interviews not only because it will help you to refine your techniques, but also for the valuable contextual data that they may reveal.

As with surveys and questionnaires, there is a sense that the strength of more structured interviews is the authoritative stability implied by their apparently systematic nature. This is debatable, nevertheless it is clear that in some contexts, very structured interviews with set questions may be appropriate. For instance, when interviewing possessed spirit mediums in northern Zimbabwe, David Lan found it necessary to:

> Establish the degree to which the answers given to questions (mine and others) by the spirits were conventionalized, the degree to which the answers would be different depending on which *mhondoro*/medium was questioned and on the circumstances in which the questioning took place. The partial solution I found to this attempt to estimate the individual creativity of the mediums was the simple expedient of asking all *mhondoro*/ mediums the same set of questions irrespective of which tradition of *mhondoro* they belonged to, as well as to put the same questions to numbers of other people whether or not they were reputed to have particular knowledge of the past of the ways of mediums, women as well as men, children as well as adults.
>
> (Lan 1985: 232)

David Lan's reasons for taking this structured approach may well relate to the unusual nature of his informants – ancestral spirits possessing mediums – and the very unclear 'agencies' that involves. His was an attempt to stabilize and bring order to a complex social/cultural situation where it was not at all clear which or whose voice was speaking. Although Lan's was a fairly unique research situation (but not *hugely*, for anthropology), and a fairly unusual approach (only partially successful), this example highlights an important point about interviews: not only can they be difficult to control, it can also be difficult to be clear about the nature of the material being elicited. This returns us to Turner's point about separating participants' interpretations from those of the anthropologist, and again emphasizes the importance of taking into account 'significant contexts'. Interviews rarely provide 'thick description', and working out the 'significant contexts' of an interview – the matters being discussed, the manner of conversation, the manner of the informant/s and the interviewer, and the assumptions embedded in his or her questions/research agenda – is vital to the interpretation of the material being generated. This returns us to a) the importance of combining research methods; and b) the importance of reflexivity about the methods and techniques you use, and the cultural, social and political assumptions embedded within your research project. As a fieldworker you should reflect upon who you are choosing to interview and why, where and how you choose to do this, and what you tell an informant about the kind of information you are looking for. This is not only about refining your techniques in the field, although that is very important; it is also about the status of the knowledge that is generated.

Box 5.1

Participatory and multimodal research methods

The strengths of ethnographic research lie in the fact that it is socially embedded and interactive rather than detached and extractive. Since different people interact, learn and express themselves in different ways, to ensure that a variety of people have a voice in your research you may need to facilitate this using a variety of participatory methods. Whereas some people will gladly tell you their autobiographies or respond eloquently to your direct questions, most will not. You may, however, learn a lot by walking with them through a village or across a landscape; constructing a model with them to depict a remembered or anticipated scenario; playing a group audio-visual activity with them (such as putting together a video or photography show) that may lead to an informal focus group discussion; or getting them to show you their pictures or possessions. 'Participatory' means involving others collaboratively in generating knowledge. 'Multimodal' means using a variety of methods and sensory channels to do this. Inspired in part by anthropology's mix of methods and by the idea of non-extractive, collaborative learning, from the 1970s development planners developed a raft of methods for facilitating participatory learning and planning, under such labels as 'Rapid Rural Appraisal' and 'Participatory Action Research'. Since then, methods and well-documented cases studies have proliferated while affordable technical support such as digital video and file sharing have become widely available. These approaches are often (though not always) associated with empowerment of disadvantaged people, and have now become mainstreamed in development organizations as ways of facilitating better communication and relationships across cultural and hierarchical divisions.

Handbooks, online guides and users' accounts of these offer lots of valuable ideas for activities that you can try out during your fieldwork. Choose carefully and try them out cautiously. Not all kinds of participatory methods will be culturally or situationally suitable; and there are risks of unrealistic expectations that research will lead to action projects and to social transformation. They may also take up a lot of time without producing much by way of recordable information. But do be patient, because enjoyable relationship-building activities may appear not to generate knowledge directly, but may be transforming you from a stranger into a trusted listener and an interesting person to engage with.

Useful references:

Clark, Alison. 2011. 'Multimodal Map Making with Young Children: Exploring Ethnographic and Participatory Methods', *Qualitative Research*, 11(3): 311–30.

Praxis – Institute for Participatory Practices (India), http://www.praxisindia.org

Eldis.org Participation Manuals, www.eldis.org/go/topics/resource-guides/manuals-and-toolkits/participation-manuals

Whyte, William F. (ed.). 1991. *Participatory Action Research*. Newbury Park, CA: Sage.

Surveys and questionnaires

Research in the social sciences is often differentiated by method, and the distinction between qualitative and quantitative methods is often assumed to be one of almost disciplinary significance. Although ethnographic fieldwork is known for its predominant emphasis on qualitative methods, quantitative approaches do often form part of an ethnographer's toolkit, and not only in 'applied research' contexts (see also Box 5.1 for information about participatory research techniques which have been a particular feature of applied/development anthropology). As we have suggested, surveys and questionnaires are sometimes attractive to fieldworkers because of the aura of 'systematic' authority and stability that they appear to offer. Like very structured interviews, these methods do not produce 'thick description' or 'deep' cultural data. They do offer other, broader (if shallower) kinds of material which may be useful as part of a toolkit of research techniques, particularly for making meaningful the kinds of data that the more qualitative research approaches discussed earlier generate. Again, there are many useful reference books available that provide good ideas about effectively using these kinds of research tools (see Chapter 2 for examples).

If, in the style of Wacquant, you wish to explore the life experiences of professional boxers, doing survey research (perhaps including some statistics) to generate data about the economic lives of the socially marginalized classes from which most professional boxers emerge, would provide some of the crucial 'significant contexts' with which we can make sense of the more qualitative data that interviewing boxers might generate. So, ethnographic fieldwork might involve quantitative research methods, and certainly anthropologists do often refer to such research done by others. Similarly, questionnaire surveys are often used in fieldwork to provide an overview of, say, a particular group's attitude to boxing or to a ritual, which may help to make sense of more particular in-depth material generated by interviews or focus group discussions. Many fieldworkers do use small-scale surveys, often early on in their fieldwork, in order to grasp an overview of their field site, and for such limited purposes they can be very useful. Some surveys are good for generating basic census-type information, the population size of an area or neighbourhood, for example, or the household composition of a particular village, and so on. Surveys are also particularly useful for comparing two or more definable variables, such as leisure activities and political membership. The same kinds of questions of feasibility apply to this kind of research (perhaps more so) as for participant observation and interviews. Surveys can be very expensive, laborious and time-consuming, and of course for many kinds of anthropology projects they will simply not produce the kind of data required.

Researchers using such quantitative techniques should be careful about the issue of statistical significance. Be aware that unless you possess good quantitative data analysis skills, uneven returns from a questionnaire or survey may be problematic for doing useful statistics. Similar kinds of practical questions apply for doing fieldwork surveys just as they do for more qualitative fieldwork methods. It is important to consider why people might be willing to participate in a survey. What kinds of questionnaire questions will elicit the kinds of answers you want? At the same time how can you avoid 'leading questions'? Asking short and clear questions is usually preferred in surveys and questionnaires, although questions that provide yes/no answers are only going to be useful in specific contexts, and are not going to provide data that may be more broadly useful. Given the inflexibility of questionnaires and surveys, it is absolutely vital that you pre-test them before you actually do them 'for real'.

On a slightly different note, in many social contexts, people are used to seeing researchers with clipboards doing surveys, or handing out questionnaires. This is often a familiar stereotype of what a social scientist does 'in the field'. In circumstances where doing some ill-defined, 'deep hanging out' might provoke unsettling questions about your presence and intentions, doing a small survey or handing out questionnaires might be a useful way of locating and identifying yourself and your research in the field. On the other hand, in contexts where 'chuggers' (charity muggers) hustle people on every street corner, this 'clipboard' identity might be best avoided!

Key points

- Different methods generate different types of data, so tailor your own combination of methods to suite your project.
- Participant observation often relies on visual or verbal data but it also allows for eliciting other kinds of perceptual and embodied knowledge. It is also good for generating questions for follow-up interviews.
- Different interview techniques, contexts and informants can produce very different kinds of interviews, so be reflexive and try different approaches.
- Surveys and questionnaires can be useful for generating basic census-like information, gaining an initial overview of your field site, or for making sense of more qualitative data generated by other methods.

Janet has little difficulty in finding some of the new vernacular embalming entrepreneurs and they seem very keen to talk to her. But the particular ritual requirements of their new Pentecostal practices mean that she will not be allowed to take part in or learn their techniques. As there seems to be a different kind of aesthetic process involved in these emergent practices, Janet is keen to get close to the bodies as they are being embalmed, even though she has heard it is a very invasive and quite disgusting process, especially for the uninitiated. Proud of their work, however, her new informants agree that she can photograph the products of their work – the embalmed corpses – and Janet agrees to do this, thinking she may in time be able to use these photographs as part of her research, although she is not yet sure quite how. She also realizes that to understand these new kinds of funerary practices and the particular aesthetics involved, she will need to understand the social and historical contexts in which the new Pentecostal movement has arisen. So, she resolves to spend a day or two a week seeking and talking to town elders and church people to try to understand how these sudden social changes have come about.

His new living and working arrangements mean that **John** is now very busy doing participant observation. But he is also growing a little concerned that this new wealth of data is too minute, and too focused on a particular kennel, rather than greyhound-racing and its relationship to gambling more generally. He resolves that on his day off he will conduct a small questionnaire survey amongst other kennels in the area who frequent the same race course. Later on he will try to follow this up with some focus group discussions with gamblers and kennel owners in order to relate the minutia of the particular to broader social processes.

Language

The issue of how we are perceived by others in the field brings us to an issue already discussed several times (see Chapters 1 and 2), but one of such significance for doing fieldwork that it bears considering briefly again here; that is, language.

If 'fieldwork' has achieved a mythical status in anthropology, then the second great anthropological myth is that anthropologists are all brilliant linguists, able to pick up whatever language their research requires, with unusual ease and fluency. Obviously this caricature does not reflect reality. Many anthropologists struggle to reach fluency in the languages of their field sites, even after many years of immersed fieldwork, and there is a question of what we mean by 'fluency' anyway. Research assistants and translators are often employed by fieldworkers, but even in such circumstances some local language knowledge and skills are essential. Language is hugely significant both in terms of the pragmatics of doing fieldwork and the quality of the ethnographic material we gather, but also in terms of the product of our labours; what we write at the end of the research. If you cannot comprehend language and communicate effectively, you cannot do effective fieldwork. Whatever (or wherever) your research project, language issues will be central; regardless of whether you are doing primary ethnographic fieldwork or basing your project on secondary literature, whether you are doing your fieldwork 'at home' or 'away'.

On a very pragmatic level, the importance of language skills for the field-worker is a question of being able to communicate. But it is also often a question of respect, of breaking barriers, of gaining access, and of building rapport. This aspect of language does not depend on linguistic abilities, or any 'natural' aptitude for learning languages. For the purposes of gaining rapport and lowering barriers with informants, making concerted but flawed efforts to speak the local tongue can be one of the fieldworker's greatest tools. It is also something that sometimes (and usefully) sets an anthropologist off from other 'foreigners' or 'strangers' (tourists, whistle-stop-development consultants, government officials, etc.) in particular field contexts. Trying hard to speak the languages of your informants is often perceived as a mark of respect, and can form the basis upon which deeply meaningful and productive fieldwork relationships are forged.

The other (and more significant) reason why language is important relates to the quality of the ethnographic material that we gather. This is as true of fieldwork done in areas where we are 'native' speakers, as it is in fieldwork done in far away places. Because so much cultural, social and political knowledge, practice, process and performance is embedded in language, and takes place through language, being constantly alert not just to what people say and in what contexts they say it, but also *how* they say it – what words or phrases they use, how they perform their language, and the subtleties of tone, flavour and expression through which language is deployed – is enormously important. For all these reasons, to pay close attention to language is perhaps the single most important piece of advice any fieldworker should receive. This applies not just to our fieldwork encounters and conversations, but also to the ways in which we record the data that we generate.

Key points

- Language is crucial because fieldwork depends on communication.
- Learning the relevant languages is also an important social ice-breaker and rapport builder.
- Language is important because so much of anthropological significance takes place through language. Be alert not just to what people say but to how they say it.

Recording information, writing fieldnotes and embodying your ethnographic stance

There are many useful reference books devoted to the mechanics of writing ethnographic fieldnotes and recording data in the field, and we advise you to glance at these as a way of thinking about the different forms and functions of notes, as you begin to develop your own style. Emerson, Fretz and Shaw's (1995) work is particularly useful, and well worth looking at. Other good examples include Sanjek (1990) and Van Maanen (1988). If you are using photography and film to record some of your encounters, events and data, you may find Pink (2007) helpful for thinking about audio-visual recording and representation.

The question of whether to tape interviews and transcribe them later or to rely on a combination of memory and brief jottings to be written up into full notes soon after, is one which often preoccupies first-time fieldworkers. Most fieldworkers have tried both, and use both for different kinds of fieldwork situations. There is no doubt that recorded interviews can lead to enormously rich and detailed data, which can help focus on the minutia of particular phrases or linguistic structures, and so on. Yet fieldworkers should also be aware of their limitations. Of course, sound recordings, and audio-visual recordings for that matter, leave out all sorts of qualitative data about the context and situation of the interview. Neither should be seen as a substitute for close observation and detailed note taking. If you record your interviews, take photographs, or record film/video, you will also need to be attentive to, and write notes about, what you observe about the ethnographic situation of the interview or encounter. There is no doubt that people, interviewers and interviewees alike, speak differently when they know they are being recorded. Anyone who has ever recorded an interview will know that people often let out a sigh of relief when the machine is switched off, and often it is after this that the most interesting information emerges. Covert recording is *never* acceptable, and you will need to think hard about whether your project really demands the depth of detail that recording interviews provides.

Apart from their effect upon the interview situation, there is also the significant matter of time. As we mention in Chapter 7, transcribing takes an enormous amount of time, particularly when translating too, and in many ethnographic contexts that time is simply not available. It has been said that transcribing an hour-long conversation takes about nine hours, while writing detailed descriptive notes from memory or jottings takes approximately three hours. Leaving recordings of interviews for transcription later risks never getting around to it, and many anthropologists' shelves contain untranscribed tapes of interviews recorded years ago. Because you will need to write descriptive contextual notes about any interview afterwards anyway, fieldworkers who begin by recording everything, often gradually find themselves recording fewer and fewer interviews as they gain confidence in their ability to recall what was being said, as their language and note taking abilities improve, and as demands upon their time increase.

It is not unusual for less experienced fieldworkers to rely heavily on recording, and this may relate to insecurities they have about their own ability to remember what was said and done during ethnographic encounters. You can train yourself to remember things better in order to write them down later on. The daily practice of writing fieldnotes is part of this self-training process, and key to becoming an accomplished fieldworker. This is a good reason why one of the first things you should do when you enter the field is begin to write notes about the things going on around you, even if they have no clear connection to what your project is focusing on. It is about training your short-term memory to remember what is going on about you, what people are saying/doing, and *how* they are saying/doing it, so that you can write rich notes afterwards. In time, many fieldworkers find that this daily remembering and note writing becomes something of an obsession. You may find you are unable to sleep until you have written your fieldnotes. It might become part of your dreams, or something you think of the moment that you wake up. It can permeate a fieldworker's very being, becoming part of the way you participate in everyday fieldwork situations. In other words, participating in a situation in order to write notes about it, is a very particular way of participating, and often becomes internalized in a fieldworker's own dispositions. This fieldwork stance, or *habitus*, is an embodied positioning or way of being, which can be subtly different to our 'normal' non-fieldwork selves. This is partly why ethnographic fieldwork has gained its mythical, transformative status, but it is also another reason why fieldwork can be so demanding and exhausting.

Of course, in between events, interviews and your daily detailed note writing, you will often have reason to make all sorts of scrappy notes, sketches, jottings and if you can, more detailed notes in shorthand. Similarly, photographing or filming video clips of people, places and events alongside these jottings may capture images and sounds that will jog your memory when you come to write your detailed fieldnotes. Never be without some paper and a pencil. Indeed, this is not only *the* alternative to recording interviews, but also a technique you might deploy at other moments during long or full fieldwork days, particularly if there is a lot going on between moments when you are able to take your time to write up full, descriptive notes.

What you write about in your fieldnotes will obviously depend on your project, the day, the events you are describing, and the stage your fieldwork is at. Once you have embodied your own fieldwork stance, you may have days where you write very little, and others where you write thousands of words. One good trick for training yourself and learning how to be in a situation about which you want to write notes, is to focus on obvious visual markers, like where in a room different people are sitting and what they are wearing, or to construct a temporal sequence of events, such as what happened or was said before person X came into the room, and what happened next, and so on. This is also a technique that can lend itself well to exploring more visual forms of recording data. Once you get used to fieldwork this becomes almost second nature, and certainly you will not need to write the same details in your notes over and over again, when such 'normal' spatial and temporal markers have become familiar. In later notes you may only write about such things when someone says, does, or wears something unusual, outside the norm that you have become accustomed to. Often, it is once these basics have been established that you will find it easier to focus on more difficult issues like the manner, tone or tense of *how* people are speaking or acting in any particular context or situation.

One important thing to consider is to keep your detailed, rich and evocative descriptions of events, utterances and situations separate from your analysis or ongoing reflections upon them. This may be in different notebooks/files, or simply in different paragraphs on a page. This can be tricky but its importance relates to the longevity of the usefulness of your fieldnotes. The same fieldnotes can serve very different purposes during and following fieldwork, in the life of your anthropology project as whole, and long afterwards. It is not unusual for the detailed descriptive parts of your fieldnotes to be important in unexpected ways long after fieldwork, while your in situ, day-to-day analysis and processing of information may be of much more immediate utility. Often, you will only know what is relevant for your final report, dissertation, or thesis long after you have come back from fieldwork. But in the midst of doing fieldwork, you will be thinking about what has been said or observed on any particular day, what leads you should follow up, what new and further questions emerge from your data as you are gathering it, and so on. Read and reflect on your fieldnotes during fieldwork (more about this in Chapter 7). These in-situ interpretations and reflections are hugely significant as fieldwork progresses, and indeed are often provoked by the very act of writing fieldnotes (a further reason for writing copiously and regularly). Fieldnotes in which the descriptive and more abstract or analytical parts are too closely intertwined might prove much less useful when you come to communicate and write up your research, when, with the benefit of hindsight, your in-situ interpretations (particularly those made early on) will often appear rather naive and ill-informed.

This points to another important issue to consider when you are writing fieldnotes. In many respects your fieldnotes will become your fieldwork. You may be surprised how little you remember, and how much you forget about your daily encounters, once your fieldwork is over. This is one reason for writing good, detailed fieldnotes. But equally important is the need to keep one eye focused on the final anthropological product that you will be producing. Thinking ahead about what might become a good quote, an organizing metaphor, or a useful case study, is critical. What might also be a useful image, video clip, or series of photographs? Think about *how* you write notes that might become quotable sections or examples in your thesis, paper, or dissertation. What tense will you write in, for example? In diary-like writing we often use the past tense, but writing in the present tense can make ethnographic descriptions much more vivid and alive. As you write fieldnotes you are already shaping the raw material with which your final anthropological product will be formed. As your fieldwork becomes your notes, their richness, depth and vividness will in part be determined by *how* you write, and the style you develop and adopt.

You will also need to organize your fieldnotes as you write. Flick forward to Chapter 7 for our advice about ways to categorize and organize your fieldnotes and audio-visual research materials. However you organize your fieldnotes it is important that you do so, because months or even years after your fieldwork, your notes will appear difficult to get a grasp upon, unless they are indexed or categorized in some way.

Finally, you will need to think about the security of your fieldnotes. Ensure you back up your notes regularly, and that you store them separately, preferably by sending them home. There is nothing more soul destroying than losing fieldnotes you have spent weeks and months collecting. They are your fieldnotes and they are irreplaceable. You may have concerns about whether to allow others access to your notes. This is your decision; sometimes it can be useful to have other people comment on and supplement your own observations. If your material is so sensitive that it could cause harm if it fell into the wrong hands, then you probably shouldn't be writing about it at all, or perhaps even doing a research project on it in the first place. However, it is also not always clear what the sensitivity of particular information may be in different contexts or in times to come (see Chapter 6 for more about these important issues). It is probably best to keep your fieldnotes as secure as possible and to avoid writing down anything that might put yourself or someone else at serious immediate risk.

Key points

- While recorded interviews can provide enormously detailed information, they also leave out other significant qualitative data. Transcribing tapes is very time consuming, and you should consider whether this is time well spent in the field.
- Train yourself and your memory in order to write rich, detailed fieldnotes. This is key to developing or embodying a fieldwork stance, so start this as soon as you arrive in the field.
- Keep your descriptive notes separate from your more abstract thoughts and reflections.

- Experiment with different styles and tenses and think about what might be usable in your final research paper, dissertation, thesis or report.
- Date, categorize and organize your fieldnotes. Keep back ups and keep them secure.

Janet is now spending a third of her time with new vernacular embalming entrepreneurs. They are very busy as more customers turn away from older funerary businesses, and as more people are killed in the deepening gang violence. This means that her interviews with them tend to be brief, and to ensure that she captures as much detail as possible, she decides to record them using her voice recorder, as well as taking photos of the embalmed corpses. She is spending quite some time transcribing the interviews, to avoid having a backlog after fieldwork, but she is also spending a lot of time writing fieldnotes about her less formal encounters with the embalmers. She is also carefully recording her experiences of learning the embalming practices and techniques that her initial hosts are teaching her during weekly sessions at their funeral parlour. She is pleased that she decided to continue working there because she has developed a good rapport with the funerary directors and their clients, and is able to converse informally with them about the broader social changes sweeping the small town. Janet has become much more disciplined in managing her own time than she ever is at home, and is surprised at how much of the day's events she can remember when she sits down to write her daily notes.

John too is finding that his fieldwork is becoming all-consuming. Living at the kennels has given him unique insights into the murky world of greyhound-racing and gambling. He is becoming increasingly aware of what appear to be legal or semi-legal gambling activities taking place at the kennels and elsewhere. He is beginning to realize that taking fieldnotes, talking to people and taking photographs are much more sensitive issues than first appeared to be the case. In order to encourage people to talk to him he has decided not to record his interviews nor to photograph his informants. With ongoing criminal investigations in and around the greyhound track, he is becoming aware that more and more people are showing an interest in his fieldnotes, despite his assurances that he has anonymized everyone. John decides to store his notes securely and regularly at his parents' home, and only keeps one day's worth of notes on his laptop at any time. Having pre-tested his questionnaire and changed some of the questions, his survey was successful. He is confident that he now has a better understanding of the complex kin and business relationships between people and dogs across different kennels frequenting the racecourse.

References

Briggs, Jean L. 1970. *Never in Anger: Portrait of an Eskimo family*. Cambridge, MA: Harvard University Press.

Emerson, Robert E., Rachel Fretz and Linda Shaw. 1995. *Writing Ethnographic Fieldnotes*. Chicago: University of Chicago Press.

Eriksen, Thomas H. 2001 (1995). *Small Places, Large Issues: An Introduction to Social and Cultural Anthropology*. 2nd edition. London: Pluto Press.

Goffman, Erving. 1989. 'On Fieldwork', *Journal of Contemporary Ethnography*, 18(2): 123–32.

Lan, David. 1985. *Guns and Rain*. Oxford: James Currey.

Pink, Sarah. 2007 (2001). *Doing Visual Ethnography*. London: Sage.

Sanjek, Roger. 1990. *Fieldnotes: The Making of Anthropology*. Ithaca: Cornell University Press.

Van Maanen, John. 1988. *Tales of the Field: On Writing Ethnography*. Chicago: University of Chicago Press.

6 Ethics

Ian Harper

An understanding of ethics – which relates to the nature of our responsibilities – is central to all that we do in social and cultural anthropology. These
responsibilities are complex and occur at every level of our research: from
when we make decisions about where and with whom to research, to how we
interact with the communities we find ourselves with, through to how we
communicate and write about our findings. Beyond this we also need to
consider our relationships with our colleagues, the discipline and the countries
where we might end up. This chapter looks at these issues through a series of
case studies, after which we pose a number of questions for you to discuss
and with which you can think through the issues at stake as you enter into the
process of being an anthropologist.

Thinking about 'ethics'

When approaching ethical concerns around undertaking a project, most of you
will think of the ethics board in the department or school where you are based.
Indeed, this is important, and as we have seen in the chapter on preparing for
fieldwork, your project has to be approved by the university and by a board.
For most of you – as you fill out the relevant forms and audit in relation to
this – it will be quite straightforward. For some, like those who want to work
on issues in health, for example, there may be other institutional boards that
have to be dealt with as well. Research performed in, or through, the National
Health Service (NHS) in the UK, or in the Health System in the US will also
have to be run through their various ethical boards as well. These may have
different ethical principles than anthropology, so if your project is to explore
health-related issues, then you will have to think this through twice, and
double the paperwork! But there is much more to ethics than the gaining of
institutional permission. While important, this is only the first, and by no
means the most important aspect of anthropological ethics.

In short, ethics is about thinking through our relationships and responsibilities. This aspect of ethics, the thinking through of the moral and political
choices that we make in our multiple encounters in the field, and more broadly
as anthropologists, should not be confused with the formalized process of
obtaining research permission from an ethical committee. While the latter

process is essential, and we all have to submit ourselves to it, it is also a part of our audit culture (Strathern 2000) and is also about the legal protection of the institution (Harper and Jiminez 2005). At best, these two arenas are not mutually exclusive, and indeed, when well done the ethical review process should assist in the thinking through of the various responsibilities and obligations we face (some of which may indeed be legal), but for the purpose of this volume they are separated out.

In the broader and political sense, ethics is central to the anthropological enterprise. Ethics raises its head in anthropology in a number of varied and different ways. Major debates in anthropology – and what better way to understand our discipline than paying attention to some of these major controversies – have sprung up in relation to our personal political engagement, our commitment to the communities we find ourselves engaged with during fieldwork, the possibility that our interlocutors might be identified and that this might be damaging to them and their reputations, and finally, the putting of anthropological research to use for military and other ends.

First, whether or not we should give primacy to a political agenda over and above the academic is a question that occupies many anthropologists, and generates discussion (Farmer 2003; Scheper-Hughes 1995; Borofsky 2005). As Scheper-Hughes has argued – should we primarily be committing ourselves towards a politics in which we align ourselves with those who are marginalized and exploited? (Read her 1995 article and see if you agree, but also read this in conjunction with the comments of those who were asked to respond to her proposition, as these tease out some of the pitfalls of doing so, and the implications of such an approach.) Whilst a number of anthropologists may see their primary responsibility as towards political engagement and social change, with the aim of making the world a better place, not all agree. Being reflexive, we might question what this does to our objectivity and impartiality, and how this might colour what we find during fieldwork. Similarly, the anthropologist and physician Paul Farmer has dedicated his life to working towards a more equitable world, and providing medical services to the poor. He uses anthropology as a way of understanding how broader forces make the poor sick and vulnerable, and uses anthropology as a means of working towards these aims, and furthering his commitment to the poor.

Second, the extent to which we place our work in the service of particular groups, particularly those faced with threats to their way of life, is another crucial question. In the United States, this issue was a major topic in the early 2000s and the debate was revitalized around the controversy of anthropologists involved in research into the Yanomami tribe in the Amazon, and the uses to which this research was put (see Borofsky 2005 for the most complete account of this). This was a complex issue, and one that involved accusations made against certain American anthropologists that they had been involved in unlawful medical research, and that as a consequence this had resulted in a number of deaths and broken a range of our ethical tenets. But this was just the start and a range of accusations followed. The resultant debates spun around the ethics of the discipline, and where our responsibilities lie during the research process and afterwards. A key issue was the use to which our writings might be put – the state used anthropological representations of the way of life of these peoples to justify certain interventions, for example. You can also visit the American Anthropological Association website (http://www.aaanet.org) to see some of these debates, and how they responded to the crisis.

A third issue is around the identification of our interlocutors and the institutions they work within, and whether this might harm them and their reputations in any way. This has become centred around the issue of informed consent for research and hiding the identity of those whom we work with. A recent case in the UK involved the development anthropologist David Mosse, and the accusations levelled against him that his writing and publications had damaged the reputation of those he researched amongst (Mosse, 2005; Mosse 2006, and see volume 21 of *Anthropology Today* for some debate on this). Again, as with the Yamomami case mentioned earlier, the value of this critical ethical event lies in the discussions that were generated. How we respond to these incidents and controversies tells us much about the core values of our discipline.

Fourth, putting anthropological research to work for the purposes of military and other ends has its detractors. Indeed, the backdrop of the Vietnam war and anthropological relationships to military intervention was the context in which the first code of ethics in the US was written and agreed to (Mills 2003). And there are currently heated debates on the military use of anthropologists in Afghanistan – several of whom have been killed – and the use of anthropologists as spies. I could go on, but suffice it to say that one way of grappling with what matters most to the discipline of anthropology, is to view it through the lens of its more controversial engagements and the consequent ethical and political discussions that ensued.

We shall discuss one final point about ethics before moving on to the case studies. In some disciplines, like medicine, informed consent has become the ethical touchstone for judging research involving human participants (Boulton and Parker 2007; this article is the introduction to an entire special edition of *Social Science and Medicine* on informed consent from many disciplinary perspectives, which you might read into further if you are particularly interested in this issue). This has certainly affected the development of anthropological ethics, and paying attention to informing our interlocutors of what our research is about, and how it might affect them, is vitally important. This is important, whether you are jotting notes, recording an interview, or filming video. Should anyone not wish to participate, then they are certainly within their rights not to do so. However, the obtaining of formal written informed consent (which may be insisted upon in some situations, for example, if you undertake research in the health sector in the UK, and have been through a hospital or other ethics board) may not always be the most appropriate way of obtaining consent. Consider the situation where members of the community may be illiterate and unable to read or sign their name? Or, where a group or community's relationship with the state may have been negatively affected by signing pieces of paper, that had far reaching legal implications of which they were unaware? These are situations where it may be inappropriate. This does not mean, however, that we do not bother to explain what we are doing, or don't iteratively engage with our interlocutors as our research unfolds. Indeed, the obtaining of the formal piece of paper, in the name of informed consent, may lead us to think that this aspect of the ethical engagement is over. More important is a consistent and sustained commitment to the 'spirit' of informed consent, one that does not make a fetish of the piece of paper, at the expense of our broader obligations and responsibilities (Harper 2007).

By now it should be becoming clearer that each ethical dilemma that we might face is unique and highly dependent on the context we find ourselves in, but this does not mean that there is no way that they can be categorized and thought through. For example, the Association of Social Anthropologists (ASA) has a series of ethical guidelines (http://www.theasa.org/ethics/guidelines.shtml). Look at these and you will see that they are framed around a series of *relations* and *responsibilities*: relations with and responsibilities towards research participants; relations with and responsibilities towards sponsors, funders and employers; relations with and responsibilities towards colleagues and the discipline; relations with own and host governments; and finally, responsibilities to the wider society. The ASA is not alone in having a code of ethics, and each country's professional body has a website dedicated to this. The American Anthropological Association (AAA), as another example, has a similar code (see http://www.aaanet.org/profdev/ethics/upload/Statement-on-Ethics-Principles-of-Professional-Responsibility.pdf). As with the ASA guidelines, these are not legally binding (membership of associations is, after all, only voluntary), but they do reflect the desire that these be used as tools for both teaching and for stimulating discussion on ethical issues. As the AAA code states in the preamble to its code:

> In a field of such complex rights, responsibilities, and involvements, it is inevitable that misunderstandings, conflicts, and the need to make difficult choices will arise. Anthropologists are responsible for grappling with such difficulties and struggling to resolve them in ways compatible with the principles stated here.
>
> (American Anthropological Association 2012: 2)

Again, we see how these are framed around the nature of our responsibilities, and as a tool for thinking through both what our obligations are and to whom we owe them.

Thus, ethical dilemmas can manifest themselves at many different levels. Some, in the field, might require immediate judgement and action. For others the ethical dilemmas may start with the writing of the dissertation and who will see this text. While some of these can generally be thought through in a leisurely fashion, the long-term implications may be much broader and less predictable.

Key points

- There may not be any 'right' answer to these questions and dilemmas – there rarely are when it comes to ethical dilemmas – but the important thing is to think through the issues and then make informed decisions about the next course of action.
- Informed consent is important, but by no means the only aspect of ethical practice while in the field.
- The Anthropological Associations have codes of ethics that have been written to help you think through the ethical issues that you might face. Familiarize yourself with these, and make use of them.
- If you do find yourself struggling with an ethical issue, it is always advisable to get in touch with your supervisor and seek help. They are there to help you think through these issues.

Dilemmas during research

Next, using these guidelines as a way of thinking through the issues at stake, let us return to John and Janet, and some of the issues that they might face during their fieldwork. Each of the subsequent examples is followed by a couple of questions to focus the discussions.

Janet's first dilemma

During the development of their research projects and proposals all the students bounced ideas around and off each other. In this year, Janet was not the only one who came up with the idea of researching into death – one of the lecturers has a very popular course on death, and this stimulated a lot of interest. However, another of the students is upset and feels that her ideas have been 'borrowed' in the development of Janet's proposal. Although this other student is planning to look at the disposal of bodies in India, she accuses Janet of plagiarism of ideas, and complains to her supervisor.

Key questions for discussion

- Does it matter if we borrow other students' ideas?
- How do we acknowledge that for many of us, the ideas we generate are in conversation and discussion with our colleagues and cohorts?

This type of accusation is far from uncommon and falls under the rubric of the responsibilities that we have to our colleagues, and our discipline. Most of the ideas we have are developed in conjunction with others and in conversation with colleagues and friends. If the ideas are developed with others, then it is right that this should be acknowledged (as a footnote, for example). However, given the importance of ethnographic data and the huge cultural and religious differences between India and Mexico, the empirical data that will be generated will be very different. We should always try and allow the findings of our fieldwork to guide the directions of the research, and both these projects will generate quite different ethnographic data. At the early planning stage there is little need to worry that there will be a crossover of ideas.

John's first dilemma

John's first dilemma comes on gaining entry into the field. He is the son of a local General Practitioner, and as such his mother is very well known in the area where he is researching. He approaches the local dog-racing track owner, and asks if he can do research. This being a small town in the rural heartland of England, he is recognized as being the 'the doctor's boy' and is granted access. He can't help but feel a little uncomfortable, as he has a suspicion that the access he is being granted is because of the standing that his mother has in the local community and that they do not want to offend her.

Key questions for discussion

- What are the pros and cons of doing fieldwork in your own home town or 'at home'?
- Should we take advantage of family or other powerful connections in assisting us to access our field sites?

There are clearly some advantages to doing fieldwork so close to home. As John is finding out, this is opening doors for him in ways that might not have happened otherwise. As he is also finding out, the webs of relationships – and the power dynamics inherent within these – that are assisting its facilitation may not allow those he is asking to say 'no'. The sense of obligation they feel may be the determining factor and assessing the balance of this will require some careful thought. If this sort of situation is one that you are uncomfortable with, then think twice before deciding to do your research near to home.

Janet's second dilemma

Janet has realized that the necessary formal processes required for getting research permission are long, tedious and seemingly endless. She has looked at the visa application forms, and been advised that she will need to affiliate with a research institution (no foreigner is allowed to do research without this) and that this might take four months. Friends in Mexico are suggesting that she just apply for a tourist visa and do the research without letting anyone know. After all, they argue, its only a dissertation for her degree, so who would really care?

Key questions for discussion

- Is it OK to 'lie' on your visa application about why you are entering the country?
- How central is the formal fieldwork to your research project, and what constitutes primary empirical data?

First, if you are going to perform formal research – with the relevant permissions – it is essential that you allow yourself enough time. Whichever country you go to this will certainly take longer than getting a tourist visa, and may require several layers of affiliation and permissions. However, not all projects are so formally arranged and in some cases the doing of ethnographic research and fieldwork is much greyer. We would not advocate 'covert' research, in the sense of performing research while consciously deceiving those you are researching into or with that you are doing something else. However, we do acknowledge that we garner our data from such a wide range of sources (including observation, reflective fieldnotes, artifacts like paper cuttings and informal conversations) and that a trip abroad could become the reflexive backdrop of a more library-based dissertation (see Chapters 1 and 5 for more on these issues). It is quite reasonable, and frequently done, to use a trip to inform the research project rather than placing primary fieldwork at the centre of the research. At M.Sc. level, for example, many students use a period of previous travel or work abroad as the foil/focus for undertaking a more library-based dissertation.

John's second dilemma

John befriends one of the regular punters at the races. He is an acquaintance (John is doing fieldwork near his home town where he was brought up), and he notices that he is looking increasingly stressed and tired. He asks if he is OK, and the man tells John that he has gambling problems, and that they seem to be out of control. He has pawned off some of his partner's jewellery – after which she moved out of the house, although no one locally knows this yet – and is heavily in debt. He has not been sleeping and continually thinks about the possibilities that with the next win he will be able to solve all his problems. It is also starting to affect his work. At this point he breaks down in tears and asks John for help.

Key questions for discussion

- Should John attempt to deal with this issue and help in solving his informant's problems?
- What are our primary responsibilities to our informants?

Clearly, John is not qualified to deal with this, but we do have a commitment to the well-being of the people we are researching amongst. The important thing here is the well-being of the research participant, and this should take precedence over the generation of data. In this case, you might seek advice from your supervisor as to what is the best course of action, and look into the various support mechanisms that are in place for helping people with this problem. If you do face an issue that is very complex, and with which you require assistance, then always contact your supervisor for advice. You do not have to face these issues alone! Nonetheless, in this case, you might suggest that, while you are not qualified to help him, he might think about seeking medical help.

Janet's third dilemma

Janet has been working in the funeral parlour for four weeks and she is finding it very difficult. She feels she hasn't yet got much good data, and is struggling with the colloquial Spanish in the area that she has ended up in. In addition, she was not really prepared for all the suffering that she is witnessing and that so many of the visitors are in states of extreme distress over the loss of their friends and family. She is feeling socially isolated and not going out much. The people who she is working with are not at all interested in the aesthetics of the beauty of death, as she had articulated in her proposal, and she feels that she is gathering little data. She dreads going into the parlour to research. What she would really like to do is travel, go on holiday, and then go home, but she feels obligated to stay on and gather more data. Increasingly low, she finds herself crying a lot for no apparent reason and has problems sleeping.

Key question for discussion

- Should Janet stay on in her field site at all costs and finish her research?

It can be that we underestimate the emotional toll that a piece of research might have on us, particularly if we are dealing with a subject such as death. It is worth thinking seriously about the potential toll that a subject might have on us. Despite our obligations and responsibilities to others in the research process, we also have responsibilities to ourselves! In particular, we are no use to anybody if we do not look after ourselves and deal with our own well-being. This is really very important. It is quite common, even when doing a short piece of fieldwork, to feel mood swings, feelings of worthlessness (in relation to the data gathering and whether the data is any good or not) and quite low. It may be that a short period away from the research will help, and that after a break you feel invigorated and ready to return to the research. If worst comes to worst, then you can always come home, and use the (partial) fieldwork as the backdrop to a dissertation that is more informed by library research.

John's third dilemma

During the course of his fieldwork, John starts to hear rumours that one of the trainers is involved in doping and feeds cocaine to some of the dogs before races. He knows this man, and he has become a key informant, telling John much of the issues and difficulties of dog training. John finds this hard to believe, but the rumours continue to circulate. In addition he realizes after a while that there is a whole economy of illegal betting going on, informally brokered and managed and that this same man is running this as a side project. One morning, there is a knock at the door of the flat and two police detectives ask if they can talk to him. They are investigating allegations into doping at the races and have been informed that he is researching into this area, and ask if he has any information which can help them with their case. In particular they would very much like to have a look at John's fieldnotes and ask if this is possible.

Key questions for discussion

- What is the balance of obligations on the one hand to your informants' privacy, and on the other to the investigation of criminal activity?
- More broadly, is our primary responsibility to the protection of our informants or to the broader public good?

While this may seem an extreme case, it is not uncommon for students to stumble across illegal activities. These might range from the minor (like workmen asking for cash for work in the UK) to the more serious (working with NGOs or groups construed by the state as being terrorists). It is very important to realize that you are bound by the laws of the country where you are researching. Failure to do so may land you in serious legal difficulties, and in some contexts, potential danger. You may be legally obliged to hand over your fieldnotes and any audio-visual material you may have. If you anticipate this as a potential problem, then there are ways in which you can deal with this. For example, the fieldnotes themselves can be written in such a way that they need a code to decipher them (Pettigrew et al. 2004). Another way is to regularly send your fieldnotes and materials home, rather than keeping them on your person. Nonetheless, your university ethics board will have a strict line on what should be done if you stumble onto illegal activities, and you should report this back to them and get legal advice.

Janet's fourth dilemma

Towards the end of her fieldwork, the area where Janet is researching erupts into social unrest. This part of Mexico has long been embroiled in a low-grade conflict between the state and drug lords. The violence increases dramatically over the period of a week, with a number of gun battles and deaths – both of police and drug peddlers. In one skirmish, several bystanders are shot and killed. A state of emergency is declared and civil liberties suspended by the state. Locally it is announced that it is best to stay indoors, and to not travel after dark or to go to areas where crowds are gathered. Janet is confused as to what to do, and wonders if it is best to leave or stay put.

Key questions for discussion

- What do you do if civil or other forms of unrest develop in your field site?
- Is this an opportunity to perform 'accidental anthropology'?

In a situation where violence and unrest breaks out, then there are several options open to you. In this situation you have to consider your safety first. It is always wise, if you are going to a place where there is known to be civil unrest, to think about this before you go, and plan possible routes of retreat as soon as you arrive. If the site is not recommended for travel by the Foreign and Commonwealth Office (UK) or State Department (USA) before you leave, then the university will not let you do the fieldwork in the first place. However, after you arrive, you must register with your local embassy. They will have recommendations as to the best course of action for you, so see what the recommendations are from them. Second, and as critical, it is really important that you ask your local contacts what to do. They will be likely to have the best on-the-ground approach and suggestions. While you should also get in touch with your supervisor at the university to ask what to do, remember that s/he is not necessarily in the best position to know what course of action to take!

John's fourth dilemma

John is writing up his dissertation and is concerned with the anonymity of his subjects. Some of the activities he has come to find out about, even if they are not illegal, could be perceived as being somewhat 'grey'. He knows that the senior managers of the racecourse have asked to see the dissertation, and have made this a condition of the research. He is worried, however, that once they see it some of the employees might get into trouble. He is having difficulty thinking how he might create enough anonymity.

Key questions for discussion

- Is anonymity of our informants the primary ethical goal of social anthropology?
- How might anonymity be achieved in this case?

Anonymity, or the hiding of the identity of our informants, is an important aspect of our writing. You can ask them if they mind if you mention them by name, and they may say that this is fine. It may be an idea to run a draft of the dissertation past them – not so that they can get you to change your interpretation – that is after all your take on the situation, and something that you should have discussed with them beforehand. It is possible that they are best situated to know whether a piece of writing may damage their employment and work relations. However, it may be that this piece of writing is too revealing of other informants in the situation you have addressed. One option is to create composite individuals – mixing up aspects of different people you met into one – to make identification more difficult. If you think that anonymity will still be difficult, as there are too few people involved, then you could anonymize the place where you did the research as well as the individuals. Alternatively, and if you have committed to showing your findings to the managers, you may have to consider only writing about and presenting some aspects of the research and not all of it. This is a difficult judgement call, but we do all write in different ways, emphasizing different aspects of our findings for different audiences. Alternatively, you may have to acknowledge that not all writing can satisfy all audiences, and that you have to offer to write a separate report for the managers instead of giving them the final dissertation.

To sum up

We have seen that ethical dilemmas and issues can arise during any of the stages of the research process, from when we are thinking about and considering what to do, to where and how we do it, to how we deal with relations in the field, to the process of writing up and how we disseminate our findings. These responsibilities are not just to our informants, but cut across varied domains, to the discipline and colleagues, to legal responsibilities of the countries we are in, and to the broader public at large. In some ways each of the situations will be unique, and not always entirely predictable. In addition there may be competing claims as to whom we are responsible to (for example, an individual who acted as an informant for us, or to those who allowed us to undertake the research in the first place – the so-called 'gate-keepers'?). Nonetheless, this does not mean that we enter into this endeavour entirely unprepared; quite the opposite, in fact. As these case studies demonstrate – and while fictional, we encounter similar situations all the time – and as the history of the discipline makes all too clear, we cannot escape ethics. Reading about these, preparing for the potential and actual ethical issues we face should be central to our practice as anthropologists. In many senses, this also takes us to the heart of our discipline.

References

American Anthropological Association. 2012. Statement on Ethics: Principles of Professional Responsibility, http://www.aaanet.org/profdev/ethics/upload/Statement-on-Ethics-Principles-of-Professional-Responsibility.pdf (accessed March 2013).

Borofsky, Robert. 2005. *Yanomami: The Fierce Controversy and What We Can Learn from It*. Berkeley: University of California Press.

Boulton, Mary and Michael Parker. 2007. 'Introduction: Informed Consent in a Changing Environment', *Social Science and Medicine*, 65(11): 2187–198.

Farmer, Paul. 2003. *Pathologies of Power: Health, Human Rights, and the New War on the Poor*. Berkeley and Los Angeles: University of California Press.

Harper, Ian. 2007. 'Translating Ethics: Researching Public Health and Medical Practices in Nepal', *Social Science and Medicine*, 65(11): 2235–247.

Harper, Ian and Alberto Corsin Jiminez. 2005. 'Towards an Interactive Professional Ethics', *Anthropology Today*, 21(6): 10–12.

Mills, David. 2003. '"Like a Horse in Blinkers": A Political History of Anthropology's Research Ethics', In P. Caplan (ed.), *The Ethics of Anthropology: Debates and Dilemmas*. New York and London: Routledge, pp. 37–54.

Mosse, David. 2005. *Cultivating Development: An Ethnography of Aid Policy and Practice*. London; Ann Arbor, MI: Pluto Press.

——2006. 'Anti-social Anthropology? Objectivity, Objection, and the Ethnography of Public Policy and Professional Communities', *Journal of the Royal Anthropological Institute*, 12(4): 935–56.

Pettigrew, Judith, Sara Shneiderman and Ian Harper. 2004. 'Relationships, Complicity and Representation: Conducting Research in Nepal during the Maoist Insurgency', *Anthropology Today*, 20(1): 20–26.

Scheper-Hughes, Nancy. 1995. 'The Primacy of the Ethical: Propositions for a Militant Anthropology', *Current Anthropology*, 36(3): 409–40.

Strathern, Marilyn (ed.) 2000. *Audit Cultures: Anthropological Studies in Accountability, Ethics and the Academy* (EASA series in Social Anthropology). London: Routledge.

7 Sorting things out

Organizing and interpreting your data

Lotte Hoek

The aim of this chapter is to help you organize and interpret the data you have gathered in the field or library. We will suggest that analysis in anthropology is an idiosyncratic practice by which you link theoretical ideas and empirical material in creative ways to make anthropological arguments. To become confident in your own analytical practice, we provide you with a number of tools that can help you order and analyze your data so you can start making your dissertation arguments.

Introduction

It can feel like drowning, returning from the field with a mass of data in apparently disconnected bits. It can be an overwhelming feeling to return after a fruitful period of fieldwork with a mass of data that appears entirely random, the bulk of it weighing down on you, snippets floating around your mind. Whether you have returned from the sites of a nearby library or a far-flung hospital, you will have collected a mountain of information. How do you start to make sense of this mass of observations, scribbled fieldnotes, typed-up conversations, photocopied paperwork, photographs and diligently collected census data? How do you organize it in such a way that you feel at least a little sense of control or overview? And how do you start to use it effectively to make anthropological arguments?

This chapter will help you make a start at sorting it all out. We will discuss ways in which you might organize your fieldwork data and give some suggestions about how to analyze it so that you can transform your data into a streamlined anthropological argument. We will not set out a series of steel analytical frameworks that can be placed, like a chicken coop, over your unwieldy data. Instead, we suggest that anthropology profits from a creative, interpretative approach to data analysis. A good anthropological dissertation effectively uses the data gathered to make a few strong analytical points in a creative and convincing manner. While it may seem that the sea of data you are submerged in will never allow itself to be transformed into such an argument, there are some practical steps you can take to gain some control over your data and to produce the distance to think creatively with it.

What is data?

Before turning to practical matters, it is important to give some thought to the ways in which data and processes of analysis have been understood in anthropology.

Early anthropologists often approached the information they gathered from their sites of fieldwork (whether myths read in library collections, dialects mapped, or skulls measured) as the equivalent of the temperature or speed measurements taken by physicists. They considered anthropology a science in search of the laws of man and society. Such laws could explain, causally and unambiguously, the ways in which societies transformed or religious thought developed. These laws could be discovered by anthropologists analyzing their systematically collected fieldwork data.

The scientistic view has largely been abandoned within contemporary anthropology. Today, few anthropologists subscribe to the view that social life can be understood in terms of universal laws or that the aim of anthropological research is to gather the raw data to insert into analytical matrices that will prove or disprove hypotheses describing causal links. Our understanding of what anthropological data is and what the possible outcomes of anthropological analysis may be have shifted in the second half of the twentieth century as our idea of anthropological knowledge and its means of production have changed.

The data that interests anthropologists, Malinowski's 'imponderabilia of everyday life', are never really 'raw', waiting to be plucked from the trees by passing anthropologists. Instead, the data we collect is always already 'cooked'. It has been interpreted, made meaningful and packaged or summarized by those who we interact with and by anthropologists who try to understand, write down and process those ideas, objects or images. 'What we call data are really our own constructions of other people's constructions of what they and their compatriots are up to' (Geertz 2003: 178). Geertz's hermeneutical approach to studying culture suggested that anthropologists shouldn't ask what a thing *is* but rather what it *means*, or how it is understood within a particular way of life. It is part of a constructionist perspective, in which access to the world is always mediated by shared ideas about its nature. From this perspective, data are always already a set of interpretations about the world.

The shift within anthropology towards a concern with meaning roughly coincided with a series of theoretical challenges within the social sciences and humanities that discouraged the view of the research process as undertaken by a disinterested scientist, gathering straightforwardly empirical data in an objective manner, untainted by personal interests or structural constraints, and analyzed transparently. Positing that knowledge is an effect of power rather than the progressive unfolding of truth, postcolonial, feminist and Marxist critiques highlighted the impossibility of anthropologists doing research from a power-neutral position outside society, as if they were not a part of the social situations under study. Instead, critics pointed out that the historical conditions of empire as well as the personal positions of individual anthropologists, marked by complex intersections of race, gender and class, impacted the sorts of research they were able to do, the type of data they gathered and the analytical perspectives they chose (Asad 1973; Rubin 1975; Wolf 1982). The anthropologist's personal and historical position, including their theoretical training, inflects the data that is gathered and their modes of analysis.

The nature of anthropological data and the personal practices of analysis are therefore not necessarily as straightforward as they may seem. Data is constructed, the anthropologist is positioned. For some, these debates may seem too abstract to be of direct relevance as they sit down with their data. For others, they may appear paralyzing as they undermine any sense of concrete data or a position from which to analyze that data. Neither should be the case. As you survey your data and start to analyze it, try to keep in mind the partial nature of that data. You can use it to say something specific, in a reflexive manner, about a particular time and place, from a specific and clearly articulated position or 'standpoint'. The locatedness of anthropological research is its strength but it also means that as you ask your data to speak, it needs to speak from that location. Keep it clear in your mind that your data is yours, that someone else would have found other things. And remember that your data speaks of particular occasions, situations, times and places, not of general laws, universal truths or timeless knowledge.

Key points

- Data doesn't exist in any 'raw' or objective form, to be collected like butterflies.
- Your own position in the world will determine how and what sort of data you collect, and the ways in which you will then analyze them. It is important to account for this position.

Janet had been well aware that her position as a middle-class, educated Briton had eased her access to the Mexican funeral parlours. During her fieldwork she had often felt uncomfortable when she was allowed to take photographs of the corpses. She instinctively felt that others would not have been given this intimate privilege but that she had been made an exception of on the basis of her outsider status. Back from the field and at her desk, she now wondered whether the pictures she had taken so reluctantly would be admissible as fieldwork data. She felt strangely guilty about the photographs and started to consider them tainted by the evident inequalities of power that had called them into being.

However, as she sat down with all her notes, Janet realized that the photographs spoke most eloquently about the perceptions of aesthetic beauty that she had set out to study. She would lose a very important part of her data if she left the photographs out. Eventually, she decided she could only include the photographs if she gave an account of the ways in which the photographs had come into being, describing both her perception of the power imbalance that had given her access as well as details about the photographic process.

Janet concluded that as long as she clearly articulated the position from which she had taken the photographs, they could be admitted as data.

John had had a productive fieldwork period and had diligently collected a vast array of primary and secondary data. But as he now surveyed his rich takings, he was beset by a feeling of futility. He wondered whether any of it was meaningful at all, rather than just a morass of constructions upon constructions. How to say anything meaningful about his data when the data itself was a construction, which referred to another construction, that he now was going to make yet another construction of? It seemed a pointlessly circuitous exercise.

While it was largely the need to complete his degree that motivated John to continue with his project, as he started to sort through his data and put it in order, he regained a sense of pleasure in the work. Even if the data was all a series of constructions, it was his construction to produce. The analysis he would create would be his story, his account of the way gamblers understood and expressed their ideas about luck. And in that partial manner, it would contribute to the understanding of gambling addiction from a very particular point of view which, even if constructed, was deeply meaningful to those people John had worked with and, by now, to John as well.

Data management: sorting stuff out

To start making sense of your data and spinning it into arguments, it is important you have a clear idea of what data you have. This means organizing it in such a way that you have a sense of overview and it becomes searchable and manageable (see also Chapter 3). Every anthropologist will have their own, idiosyncratic, ways of managing and filing the data, and like fieldwork, this way of working isn't always transparent to others. This is not necessarily a problem, as long as you can find your own way around the notebooks, tapes, documents and clippings.

For most anthropologists, data collection is complete when they return from the field or library and are back behind their desks. It is becoming increasingly easy to continue data collection from behind that desk though, with the access to archives online, mobile telephones, email and other forms of media technology. While this might seem like an advantage, and occasionally may be so, there are good reasons to draw a definite line under the process of data collection. There is a potentially infinite amount of data you may collect on your topic. If you do not draw a line, you will not be in a position to start the process of constructing your arguments and writing up. Instead, there is a real danger that your project won't come to an end at all if you give in to the temptation to keep on collecting. Stick to the timeframe you set for yourself in your research proposal, your project will be the better for it.

Once you have drawn a line under the process of data collection, you will find yourself with a vast collection of diverse forms of data: a notebook containing quickly scribbled fragments, sketches, citations or further references; digital copies of photographs, scans, audio and video recordings; files full of newspaper clippings, documents and photocopies; written out life histories; numbers and census data; and perhaps a digital or handwritten document in which those scraps of data have been more or less narrativized into a readable account of the fieldwork. The first thing to do is to get a clear but rough sense of what sorts of data you have. Make a list, note down the bits and pieces you have collected. This does not have to be a detailed account of what is *in* those diverse sources. Instead, it is a first organizational level that gives you a sense of control over the data. Later on it may also help you remember that bag of flyers you had collected but that had sat forgotten on a shelf while you had delved into your interview data.

Once you have a sense of what forms of data you have, the next big step is to start to get a sense of what is in that data. There are many ways to do this, and mostly you'll have a pretty good idea of the important anecdotes, excellent interviews or useful headlines you want to use. Nonetheless, going through all your data in a structured manner will bring to light forgotten incidents or unsuspected bits of data. It is important to set aside a good chunk of time for this process, which can be quite tedious and is hard work. I'll discuss a few common forms of data and suggest ways in which they can be opened up and made searchable.

Fieldnotes

The main container of your data will probably be your fieldnotes. These describe in meticulous, and often suffocating, detail the time spent on the research. It isn't necessarily a fun task but it is important that you *read* your own fieldnotes. Do so with concentration and take enough time to do the task thoroughly. It is tempting to briefly scan your notes, you are the author after all, what revelations can they possibly hold? But you'd be surprised at how much you will already have forgotten or simply hadn't realized the import of. Even when your research period is short, perhaps only six weeks in the field or library, but especially if you are doing a long stretch of research, such as for a Ph.D. thesis, it is worthwhile to set aside time while in the process of research and afterwards to read your notes through. Giving you time to reflect on the data already collected, its relevance and its gaps, reading through your field-notes at intervals will give you a good sense of your data and its general trends, as well as pointing to new directions for data collection. In the literature on 'grounded theory', this is called 'constant comparison', drawing attention to the simultaneous nature of data collection and analysis (Glaser and Strauss 1967). It might also give you a break from the demands of fieldwork, and an escape from the library or archive, to a nearby oasis of some sort.

While reading your notes, you'll notice the recurrence of particular persons, notions, Gods, dates or events. There might also be singular events or anec-dotes that stand out, perhaps with little relation to the other events and con-versations written down in your notes. To be able to track where these occur it can be helpful to produce an index for your notes. Very much like the index at the back of a scholarly book, an index makes your notes searchable and gives you an immediate overview of the mention of persons, organizations, concepts or places. This does require your fieldnotes to have page numbers and perhaps volume numbers, so you can refer to concrete places in your notes (for example, 'notebook 3, page 76' or 'Word document "Fieldnotes May 2012", page 4'). While you are reading through your fieldnotes, keep a separate notebook at hand where you can jot down the places in which terms appear that seem relevant to you. You can sort these into an alphabetic index that you can add to as you continue to read. The entries you deem significant will undoubtedly shift over the course of the project and keeping your index updated will reflect this. Having a well-organized index unlocks your fieldnotes for analysis and writing up.

Recorded interviews and focus groups

If there is one form of data management that is almost universally considered a pain in the backside, it is the transcription of recorded interviews. What took only ten minutes to discuss, will take you at least an hour to transcribe. It is a laborious and often tedious process. Nonetheless, accurately transcribed interviews to read through and to quote in your writing are among the best resources for any research project in anthropology. It is therefore important to transcribe recorded interviews in a timely, judicious and faithful manner. Don't underestimate the amount of time it will cost to transcribe your recordings and factor this into your timetable.

When starting on the transcription of an interview, especially if some time has elapsed since you made the recording, it is worthwhile to listen through the entire interview first. Roughly note what themes are discussed and give time codes for where these themes occur. It is unlikely that everything in the interview is of equal relevance and you may choose to only transcribe in detail those points at which the most relevant themes occur. Once you have transcribed the interviews to your satisfaction, the written documents can be indexed.

You will encounter plenty of problems in transcription. Whose voice are you hearing? What is being said when two or more people speak all at once? Besides patience as you rewind again and again, until an unclear statement becomes meaningless sound, you might ask someone else to listen to particularly obstinate bits of recording. You might also find it useful to use digital audio editing software such as Audacity (available for free online), to slow down the speed of your digital recordings. Reconcile yourself to the fact that some bits of audio will inevitably sink into total opacity as you fail to make meaning of it. This is inevitable and a reminder that recording interviews is no guarantee of concrete and reproducible data.

Documents and clippings

During your fieldwork you may have gathered a significant body of secondary data. Newspaper and magazine clippings, documents from organizations or institutions, reports and statutes, flyers and advertisements, the list is endless. You can sort your collection of documents according to type. Then lay them out chronologically or any other sequential or hierarchical ranking you find meaningful. You will need to devise a system to refer to these various documents if you want to use them in your written dissertation and organizing them will help you do so, as well as producing clarity in the collections. As with the fieldnotes and transcribed interviews, you can index the documents you have gathered.

You might have done fieldwork in a place where people speak and write a language you are not completely in control of. In that case, it is helpful to mark up each of the documents in a language you are comfortable with, noting briefly what the content of the document is, perhaps underscoring a particular segment, and noting its author, publisher, place and date of publication, if applicable. Once you come to doing an analysis, you will be able to quickly flip through the documents without having to painstakingly translate each sentence.

Images: still and moving

As advanced photography and video applications are now embedded in mobile phones, and freeware editing programs widely available, more and more anthropologists are starting to use (audio-) visual technologies as part of their data collection. Photographing people and places, videoing events, scanning pictures, you will have a stash of images on your hard drive. Edit the photographs to a manageable set consisting of those which you might reasonably be able to, or want to, use in your research. To organize digital images, date their extensions when you save them and make sure you know when, where and of what and whom the images are.

Your wealth of visual material should not only be considered a series of illustrations. Video and still images are sources of data in their own right. To unlock this data, you might want to code your videos and images. Like indexing written text, coding imagery consists of attributing certain values to the image surface. You might mark the appearance of people, symbols, or colours in an image. You might also code the aesthetic properties of the content of the image or the image itself. The aim is to explicate the properties of particular images and videos. There are many layers of coding you can attribute to images, and it is important you do so judiciously, keeping in mind your research question. It is also important to think about questions of consent from those in visual material when you use images in your analysis and outputs.

Box 7.1

Qualitative data analysis programs

There are many software programs available that can help you with the process of analyzing your qualitative data. Known as Computer Assisted Qualitative Data Analysis or CAQDAS, programs such as Atlas.ti, NVivo, Nudist or Ethnographer are used to manage and code data. It does require all your data to be available in a digital format and in particular languages for it to function. The advantage of using software like this is that it allows you to do complex and rapid searches across your material while archiving your data in a central system. You can also count incidences of particular terms, map these and move through your data from one incidence to another.

The collective name for this sort of software is, however, misleading. While they are known as programs for 'analysis', they help you with analysis only to the extent that the practice of coding is a first step in the process of analysis. But attributing codes and making sense of them later is something you ultimately have to do yourself.

Key points

- Make sure you have a clear overview of the types of data you have.
- Unlock your data by indexing, coding, annotating and marking the texts, sounds and images you have collected.

Having decided her photographs could be included as data, **Janet** wondered what to do with them. They could nicely, if lugubriously, illustrate her dissertation. But Janet felt they could be put to better use and be integrated into her actual argument. To start with she had to somehow organize the photographs to decide which were the most helpful. To do this, she decided to code the photographs and see what emerged. Taking the pictures as faithful documents of the aesthetic values placed on the appearance of corpses, she started to make notes of the specificities of the make-up that had been applied. Listing the different parts of the body and making a note of colours, densities and positions, she systematically mapped the photos. She found the practical task a justifiable form of procrastination from the dreary work of transcription, which was taking her hours. However, as she coded more and more photographs, she started to see patterns appear. If she could illustrate those patterns by providing a sample of photographs in which those patterns appeared most clearly, she would have a visual line of argumentation to support her written text. She was glad she hadn't dismissed her photographs.

John had returned with reams and reams of documents about gambling. With gambling addiction on the rise in the region, he had found a series of research papers and policy plans at the local council. While these papers addressed directly the ostensible topic of his research, as he ploughed through the drearily written documentation, he felt they said less and less of direct relevance. While he was studying gambling, it was the question of luck that he was really interested in. And on this topic the papers were entirely silent. As he marked the documents, the term 'luck' didn't appear once, and in his index the term appeared only to refer to his interviews and fieldnotes. He concluded that the question of luck, so important to his informants and intriguing to himself, was of no interest to the concerned council representatives and policy makers. John felt this might in itself be meaningful.

Interpreting your data

While fieldwork is widely acknowledged as the mystical rite of passage of anthropology, it is often analysis that remains truly in the dark. Few anthropologists give accounts of the ways in which they come to their conclusions, how they link data to theory and how they analyze their fieldnotes. This is the underbelly of anthropology that, unlike fieldwork methods, cannot be protected by the *non-sequitur* 'I was there'.

The obscure practices of anthropological analysis have been a target of critique, both within and outside the discipline. Influential anthropologists such as Claude Lévi-Strauss and Clifford Geertz have been accused explicitly for their obscure and highly personalized methods of analysis, opaque to others. Borrowing, like magpies, from a range of methods associated with disciplines across the social sciences and humanities, anthropological methods of analysis are diverse and used in idiosyncratic ways. Rather than a weakness, the creativity and serendipity of such personalized analytical modes can be seen as a strength of the anthropological tradition, allowing for flexibility and new ideas.

Such a disciplinary tradition doesn't make for convenient analytical models or reproducible formats. Instead, as a student of anthropology you will need to find your own way towards analyzing your data. You will need to combine a good grasp of your data and an understanding of the theoretical literature with ethnographic good sense and some creative thinking. The challenge of anthropological analysis is to bind theory and data in imaginative, insightful and meaningful ways. While this cannot be taught in a straightforward manner, there are some steps you can take to cultivating such an analytical state of mind.

Knowing and using the relevant literature

Much of the specificity of anthropological modes of analysis comes from their embeddedness within a particular body of literature. This provides an analytical vocabulary and a series of concepts that you should be able to put to use in your own understanding of your data. Most likely, you will have made this anthropological vocabulary your own as you completed your coursework and prepared a literature review for your research proposal. Part of analysis is phrasing your own concerns within these vocabularies and conceptual structures. This means raising your empirical material to a level of abstraction so that the prayer service you observed in a Catholic church in your fieldwork area comes to be rephrased as 'devotional practice' or the elegant manner in which the women at the organization you worked with dressed can be understood as the 'materialization of a professional habitus'. While this rephrasing seems to simultaneously add nothing to what you could describe much more plainly, and to draw highly specific practices and objects onto a plane of generalization that erases their distinctiveness, this is part of the analytical procedure by which anthropological meaning is made. It is a legacy of anthropology's early comparative method, by which practices and ideas far dispersed could be brought into meaningful conversation. This is what you try to do as you proceed to analyzing your material. Indexing your notes, interviews and documents is part of this process as you assign more general values, very often concepts, to particular bits of data.

What the relevant terms and concepts are for your project, will emerge from the secondary literature you position your work in. The concepts and terminology you will gradually start using are most likely part of more or less clearly articulated theoretical frameworks. These theoretical perspectives set the parameters for analysis, and will already have had a part to play in how you conducted your fieldwork and research (see Chapter 4). Most anthropologists assemble an analysis from a range of perspectives, combined according to their own needs and interests. However, it is important to understand that particular bits of literature fall roughly within broad theoretical fields or schools that are based around certain assumptions and questions.

Of course, it is entirely possible to reject or tweak the terms you receive from your anthropological interlocutors. As long as you do so explicitly, explaining why you do not find particular concepts helpful, you are contributing to the lively debates in anthropology. It is these debates that you are getting into as you review your literature and start to frame your data within its concepts and categories.

Practical analytical steps

Even if you do have a sense of the main bodies of literature that speak to your project and you have a good overview of your various bits of data, analyzing this data so that it speaks to the literature can be difficult. Keeping engaged with the data, indexing and coding your material and asking yourself how it relates to the literature is a good way to keep the process of analysis going. Beyond this, there are a number of practical steps you can take to push your analytical process.

Significant events or ideas

Most anthropologists come back from field research or library research with a number of anecdotes, quotes, catchphrases or stories at the forefront of their mind. They are used as much to regale friends as to convince supervisors of the hard work undertaken. Your description of these significant events or ideas is already an interpretation, and with that, a step towards analysis. Now that you have a little more distance from its occurrence or discovery, try to think what it is about a particular statement or incident that has made it lodge itself in your mind? Why was it funny, scary, surprising or memorable? If you take the time to figure out why it has struck you as significant, you'll probably find it speaks to your research questions in a particular way. Getting clear how it does so, is part of its analysis.

Vignette writing

In your fieldnotes, you will have written out some events or concerns in a more or less narrative fashion. These may be the significant events mentioned earlier, or accounts of the ordinary and everyday goings-on at your site of fieldwork. You can now try to write these out in the more condensed version of the ethnographic vignette. A vignette is a short narrative account that pithily posits relevant details of your research. This can be the account of a single event or be a consolidation of weeks of observation of a single process, site or practice. The analytical traction of the vignette is that it condenses observations from your research in such a way that it immediately communicates what is important about a complex situation beyond its mere description. And if you can articulate the importance of that event, practice, or set of ideas, that means you are providing an analysis of it.

Recurring themes

As you make your way through your notes and other bits of data, you'll probably come across a number of recurring names, anecdotes, myths, phrases or gossip. Make a list of these. Try to think why they are so central to your observations or your fieldwork participants' lives.

Visualization

To get some grip on the complex relations among people, the layout of places, the chronology of events or the structure of organizations, visualize these in drawings or maps. These can take any form, from associative mind-maps to detailed kinship graphs. Juxtaposing the different maps of related sets of people and places can shed new light on the relations between them.

Paradoxes

Anthropological projects often come to be phrased in terms of contradictions that fieldwork data show to be mere paradoxes. What was the contradiction that you set out to study? Was it a contradiction at all or did it turn out to be a paradox? How can you suggest that what seemed a contradictory notion or practice is in fact not contradictory at all?

Doxa

Although this is often difficult, it is worthwhile trying to think about the themes your fieldwork participants didn't raise or aren't mentioned in the monographs you reviewed. There will always be practices or ideas that are so common, they go without comment. You might have been struck by some things that seemed peculiar or significant but when you tried to ask or read up about these, you didn't get very far. It is like asking Britons why their teabags don't have strings. Such a question has no real everyday explanation that you can easily jot down. It points to things that are so quotidian and deeply rooted in the way in which people experience the world, that they go without saying. Try and get a sense of what this 'doxa' is in relation to your research theme.

Idea log

As you engage more and more deeply with your data, you'll notice it will come to occupy your mind in a peculiar manner. When you aren't at all thinking of your dissertation, but having a chat in the pub or cutting up some vegetables for your dinner, suddenly an idea will come to you. Keep an idea log to keep track of these thoughts and connections. Like a field diary, it allows you quickly to note down ideas, links, or insight when they occur. Although you'll probably reject most of them as you get down to building your arguments, you can never have too many ideas.

Box 7.2

Analyzing quantitative data

If you have gathered census data, counted incidences or collected other quantitative data in your project, you need to be sure that you are able to read and compute these numbers effectively. It is crucial that you are familiar with basics of statistical analysis and conventions. You can use software programs such as SPSS to help you compute your own statistics. There are plenty of useful guides to help you with this (see further readings for this chapter). As with CAQDAS programs, the usefulness of the software will always depend on how you analyze and make sense of your material, not a machine.

Missing data

As you analyze your data and start to build your arguments, you will run into an inevitable problem. From the mass of data, a clear line of analysis is emerging! It is all looking good. And then, as you try select the bits of data that will go into a crucial vignette, terror strikes. The one piece of data that you really, really need isn't there! You read through the interview you were banking on and it isn't exactly as you thought it was. Or you realize that you never actually asked anyone about a particular thing. Or you ran out of time. Most anthropologists will at some point long for such golden but missing data. What now?

Few field sites are so remote today that they cannot be reached by mobile phones and the library will open again after the weekend. However, while some minor bits of data may be collected in such a post-fact manner, this rarely solves the problem or leads to good quality data. Instead, it will probably pay off to sit with your material and ask why you are focusing on this bit of missing data. What is it that you want to say through it? Can there be other ways in which you can resolve your apparent dead-end? Revisit the data that you do have and try to work towards your conclusions again. The missing data is often a fantasy, a form of mental block rather than a real lack of data.

Key points

- Anthropological analysis is often unsystematic and is a creative practice of linking theory and data in meaningful ways.
- You are better informed about anthropological theory than you think.
- Keep asking yourself how your data relates to the literature you have read.
- Missing data is often a fantasy.

As part of her literature review, **Janet** had thoroughly studied the literature on the anthropology of death. As she worked through her data, and condensed it into significant episodes and vignettes, she realized that her data spoke much more to questions of aesthetics than to the sort of questions dealt with in the anthropology of death. Should she just drop that body of literature? Her advisor suggested she try to understand why the literature on death didn't match her data. If she could find this out, she could make an argument about that literature on the basis of her own data.

John had started out his research wondering how gamblers could possibly hold on to notions of good luck when in fact they were mostly confronted with bad luck as they kept losing their bets. While this was an obvious contradiction to John, after collecting his data and sitting down to look at the recurrent use of the notion of luck in his fieldnotes, he realized that it had only seemed like a contradiction to him from the outside. From his conversations with the gamblers at the dog races, it now appeared that the notion of good luck was in fact predicated on the incidence of bad luck. His gamblers could only really win if they experienced loss. Rather than a contradiction, it was a paradox that told John a lot about how his gamblers understood good luck and persisted in their gambling. Setting out why there was no contradiction in holding on to notions of good luck in the face of overwhelming evidence to the contrary became central to John's analysis.

Articulating your analysis: linking data and theory

The final aim of your data analysis is to make a conceptual argument on the basis of your empirical material. A good anthropological argument links data and theory in an insightful manner. You should now be in control of your theoretical literature as well as having lifted your data to higher levels of abstraction through various practical analytical steps. You can now put these two together to make analytical arguments.

A good analysis is a specific analysis. But articulating clearly what you are after is often more easily said than done. Instead, you'll have a vague sense of what you are interested in. In drafts of chapters and research presentations this might be the most overused phrase: 'it is very interesting'. But unless you are able to articulate *why* something is interesting, it is meaningless. Phrasing your interest within a set of concepts allows you to make clear what is interesting about an empirical object.

Let's take the Nuer cows that feature so elaborately in Evans-Pritchard's work (1969) as an example. These cows are not interesting per se, not even to a biologist. The cow is only interesting if you are asking a particular question of that cow, if you are arguing about the cow because it stands for something larger. Such questions (Who owns this cow? What does it eat? Who tends this cow? etc.) already presuppose particular theoretical frameworks and concepts. For anthropologist A who asks about the ownership of the cow, the cow is interesting because it is the girls who tend the cows but the boys who will own them and therefore the cows are a peg in the gendered division of labour and patterns of inheritance among the Nuer. For anthropologist B the cow may be interesting because it is key to the maintenance of the balanced diet and calorie count within the natural environment in which the Nuer live. But for anthropologist C the cow is interesting because the cow explains why Nuer society does not fall apart despite the fact that there is no centralized government: the cows need to be fed in periods of draught and so the Nuer migrate, establishing flexible notions of time and space, which lead to a perception of kinship relations and territorial relations that are flexible, thus becoming the elastic bands that hold Nuer society together (Evans-Pritchard 1969). Note that all three anthropologists start with the same empirical cow, but analyze it in radically different manners due to the different questions they ask of it.

In all these examples, the real, complex, *empirical* qualities of the cow (its ownership, its furriness or number of stomachs) are used to say something in a more general *conceptual* manner. This is what the analysis of your empirical material aims to do. You want to participate in the theoretical debates in the literature you have reviewed on the basis of the empirical material you have gathered. While ethnography often seems to be just a series of descriptions, a bunch of fieldnotes bound and published, in fact good ethnography is empirical material organized in such a manner that it posits certain conceptual ideas in relation to the ideas of others. When you analyze your material, you are looking out for the ways in which your material speaks to the theoretical debates you are participating in. Your analysis will ultimately address large social scientific questions (about agency, or gender, religious belief or nationalism) from a very specific location, a single empirical cow.

Key points

- Your analysis is the beginning of articulating your argument.
- Make sure you are able to articulate *why* something is interesting.
- Use your empirical material to address more general social scientific questions.

References

Asad, Talal (ed.). 1973. *Anthropology and the Colonial Encounter*. London: Ithaca Press.

Evans-Pritchard, E. E. 1969 (1940). *The Nuer*. Oxford: Oxford University Press.

Geertz, Clifford. 2003 (1973). *The Interpretation of Cultures*. London: Fontana Press.

Glaser, B. G. and A. L. Strauss. 1967. *The Discovery of Grounded Theory: Strategies for Qualitative Research*. New York: Aldine.

Rubin, Gayle. 1975. 'The Traffic in Women: Notes on the Political Economy of Sex'. In Rayna Reiter (ed.), *Toward an Anthropology of Women*. New York: Monthly Review Press, pp. 157–210.

Wolf, Eric. 1982. *Europe and the People Without History*. Berkeley: University of California Press.

8 Communicating the research and writing up

John Harries

This chapter is about 'writing up' your dissertation. In so doing you will be composing an anthropological argument. This composition will emerge from all the work you have done before and that has been discussed in previous chapters: the fieldwork, the archival research and reading, and the analysis. In writing a chapter on writing up a dissertation in anthropology we will not be going into a lot of detail concerning the nuts and bolts of grammar, spelling and matter of style (although you can find a bit of that on our website). What we will do is make some suggestions about how to take all the work you have done and make it into a written document suitable for submission.

Introduction

Writing up is difficult. It is difficult for a good reason. It is difficult because you are trying to say something about something. Furthermore, that something which you are writing about is real. It exists beyond the words on the page. It even exists beyond your authorial imagination and the experience of the researcher. For example, João Biehl writes of Catarina who, in the time he knew her, lived mostly in Vita, a rundown facility for the abandoned and mentally ill who dwelt at the margins of Brazilian society. In telling her story he tells us about big issues; he seeks to 'understand how economic globalization, state and medical reform, and the acceleration of claims to human rights and citizenship coincide with and impinge on a local production of social death' (2005: 23). Yet, to speak of these big issues he needs Vita. He needs Catarina. He needs her to be real before and beyond anything he writes and any sense or significance his writing lends to her life.

Sometimes we anthropologists have claimed otherwise. We have suggested that ethnographic realism is but a way of writing, an authorial conceit which obscures the very fact that the 'reality' of others is constituted in the act of writing. So some have suggested we turn inward to critically reflect on our own authorial practices and the textual strategies by which we secure a reality beyond the text (c.f. Marcus and Cushman 1982; Boon 1982; Clifford and Marcus 1986). This critique of anthropological writing should not be dismissed lightly. It raised many important questions about how we write the lives of others. Nonetheless, we will follow the likes of Jonathan Spencer (1989) and Martyn Hammersley (1998: 56–64) and suggest that what makes our writings anthropological is precisely their relationship to human existence, vital, various and fundamentally *real*.

It is true we know these other people only in the published writings of anthropologists. Yet we trust that they have lived beyond writing. We also suspect that their lives are more prosaic and also more wonderful than anything the anthropologist writes. This is why anthropological writing is difficult. In writing you are taking the messy reality of lived existence and making it orderly to be able to say something substantive and valid about the nature of lived existence.

Our job in 'writing up' is not to communicate the quality of lived reality. Our job is to make sense of lived reality. Moreover, this sense is fashioned through a linear narrative, a chain of words progressing from left to right and from front to back. Paloma Gay y Blasco and Huon Wardle summarize this tension nicely. Writing, they argue, is 'sequential', while 'social life as it is lived, is multi-stranded and multi-dimensional' (2007: 96). To make an argument in writing is to render this multidimensional reality into a linear narrative which addresses issues which are at once imminent within that reality yet greater than it.

Writing is inherently inadequate to communicating the reality of the lives of others. Yet we write. We write in part because, despite its inadequacies, writing, along with anthropological film and photography, is the most effective medium we have of communicating the nature of the lives of others. To write about 'writing up' is to describe ways in which we create such an account.

Writing and communicating (or getting a good grade)

The key to this is communicating. You are not just trying to say something about something. You are also trying to say this to someone else. 'Writing up', as Roy Ellen reminds us, 'is a transformation of data from the category of "what you know" into a new category: "what you communicate"' (1984: 295). So, writing is not just a means of building an argument. It is also the way you relate this argument to others.

The main implication of this observation is that you must consider your audience. Potentially in anthropology there may be all kinds of others you are writing for. As students you are, however, writing for more senior academics who will be evaluating the quality of your work. In short, you want to write a dissertation that will get a good grade.

In all likelihood your university will have published a description of the criteria by which a dissertation, or any piece of written work, is assessed. It is, therefore, well worth familiarizing yourself with these grade descriptors when writing up your dissertation. They will at least give you some idea of what expectations your readers will bring to your text.

We would suggest, however, that there are two basic criteria by which the quality of your argument and dissertation will be judged:

1. Does the argument you are presenting seem to be plausible and credible?

We will discuss how you compose a plausible and credible argument a bit later on. For the moment let us say this: at the heart of your dissertation will be a series of claims about the nature of reality. These will be grounded in the lives of a real and specific group of people, but they will also aspire to speak to broader issues that exceed the peculiarities of these lives. These claims should be supported by evidence; whether that is the evidence of your own ethnographic fieldwork, or evidence gathered otherwise (through secondary reading, or archival research, etc.), or evidence that you assume supports the claims made by other credible academic authors.

2. How is the argument you are presenting relevant to anthropology?

This seems an unhelpful thing to say; however, let us work from the following assumption: as a discipline anthropology is constituted by a heterogeneous set of concerns. These concerns do not exist out there in the anthropological atmosphere. They exist in books, chapters and articles written by anthropologists. So the question 'how is the argument you are presenting relevant to anthropology?' may be translated as 'in what ways does the argument you are presenting relate to stuff that has already been written by anthropologists?' In other words, your dissertation becomes relevant by integrating the writings of other anthropologists into your writing and situating your arguments in relation to these writings. Of course, you may well incorporate the writings of non-anthropologists into your dissertation. They may indeed play an important role, especially, though not exclusively, when it comes to theorizing positions that are under-theorized within the anthropological literature. If you are writing as an anthropologist for anthropologists you must, however, account for the relevance of your argument for and within existing discussions within the anthropological literature.

The important thing to realize is that your argument is only communicated in writing. The plausibility, credibility and relevance of your argument are constituted throughout the course of the research process that has been described in previous chapters. A good argument does not just spring into being as the words emerge from the blank white page. A good argument is the culmination of all the work that came before.

So how do you go about doing such a thing? It is hard to say. There is no paint-by-numbers guide to the composition of a good, dissertation-length, anthropological argument. What we can do is make a few suggestions and provide a few hints, many of which have been drawn from our own experience of the joys and difficulties of saying something about something to someone else in anthropology.

Key points

- In writing you are communicating ideas to a readership.
- This readership will judge the quality of your work according to the plausibility and credibility of your arguments and their relevance to anthropology.
- The plausibility, credibility and relevance of your arguments are only known in the writing, but are constituted through the entirety of the research process.

The idea of writing a dissertation filled **Janet** with dread. She had found it difficult enough writing essays of only a few thousand words and with a set topic. Now she had to set the topic herself, and from all her notes and reading, her analysis of photographs and her time spent in the field she had to say something about death, the body, aesthetics and what went on in Mexican funeral parlours. It seemed impossible. More than anything she felt she did not know enough. When she read the works of other anthropologists she was impressed by how well they seemed to know the people about whom they wrote. In comparison it seemed she had done almost nothing. Sure, she had a lot of photographs and some notebooks filled with descriptions of what went on during her months in Mexico. She had spent some days and weeks in funeral parlours and attended a few funerals, but really she felt she knew almost nothing of the thoughts, feelings and lives of the people about whom she was to write. How could she turn her pile of photographs and fieldnotes, now analyzed and coded, into a dissertation?

John felt ready. From his analysis he had the basic point of his dissertation clear in his mind. This was a dissertation about luck and, as luck would have it, this was a topic that was largely ignored in much of the writing about gambling. So not only did he have a focus, but his focus seemed to address a gap in the literature, which he had been told was exactly what original research should do. Usually, he was very organized when it came to writing his essays, starting in good time, working to an outline and finishing with a minimum of fuss. This time, however, he was having trouble. He had so much material and so much of it was about luck. The idea of luck seemed pervasive. It ran through everything. How was he to sort this tangle of associations into a nice, neat argument that flowed from one point to another point and finally said something complex and interesting about luck, gambling and greyhound-racing?

Getting started

The prospect of writing a dissertation can leave one feeling a bit daunted. Some of us, like John, feel that there is just too much. The reality one wants to describe is too complex and multidimensional to ever be transformed into a tidy, linear argument. We feel that our experience exceeds any project of writing. Others, like Janet, may feel that we just don't have enough to say anything much about anything. We feel that our experience is insufficient to any project of writing. There can be some merit to the latter concern. It is hard to make something out of nothing. But most of us have a great deal more than nothing. It is just that when faced with the project of writing we can become aware of all we don't know; all those articles unread and questions unasked.

To some extent you will already have focused on particular themes and concepts as you organized, analyzed and interpreted your materials, and begun to link your empirical data with theory in interesting and insightful ways.

Free-writing

So how does one overcome these feelings and get started? There are no easy answers. Everyone has their own way of doing things. Some of us have a tendency to plunge in. We have a rough idea of what it is we want to say, we gather all our notes, coded transcripts, quotes and articles, and we just go for it. There is something to be said for this approach. 'Free-writing' is one way of describing this technique. It is, as Rowena Murray, suggests 'the opposite of knowing what you are going to say first and writing about it second' (2006: 88). Instead, we discover what we are going to say in the act of writing. Free-writing can get us over our initial inhibition concerning putting our thoughts into words. It also allows us to get some flow as we just let the words come.

The drawbacks of this approach are, however, obvious. If you launch yourself headlong into writing a paper of a few thousand words, let alone a dissertation which will likely be in excess of 10,000 words, you will soon get lost. You will write and write and the words may flow, but they are flowing all over the place rather than the orderly flow of an argument which is what we want.

Free-writing, its exponents suggest, is best done in short bursts. You write without stopping for five, 15 minutes, maybe half an hour. Free-writing is for those times when we seek inspiration by switching off our inner editor and letting the weird alchemy of the act of writing create ideas. It is not a way to set about writing an entire dissertation. To write a dissertation you need a plan and you need to write to that plan.

Planning to write

Everyone likes a plan but a plan does not make for a good dissertation; a plan enables you to write. It enables you to move forward in an orderly fashion: to know where to start, to know where to end, to have some idea of what goes where and what follows on from what. The point is not to get too hung-up about plans. Writing is, after all, a creative process. However, you do need to have some idea where you are going and how you will know when you have reached your destination.

It goes without saying, there is no single technique for planning a dissertation. One way to think about this is to return to the problem of how to render the 'messy and multi-dimensional' nature of reality into an orderly linear narrative that works from specific situations and events to speak to issues of more general concern. The trick is that in doing this you want the narrative to somehow emerge from all that you have done, read and written so far. So let us try some practical steps:

Revisit and revise your research topic

Many months ago you wrote a proposal. In this proposal you described a research topic and why this topic is interesting and worthy of study. A lot has happened since and your original ideas concerning what is significant and interesting about the lives of others will have changed through the course of your research, reading and analysis.

The first thing to do is to revisit your proposal and rewrite your research topic. Keep this quick and simple. Do a bit of free-writing. Begin with the phrase 'This dissertation is about ... ' and write for ten or 15 minutes without stopping. You should have a short paragraph. Then take this topic, ponder a bit and have another go at free-writing, this time beginning with the phrase 'the central question that will be addressed in this dissertation is ... ' and rephrase your research topic as a question. Have a look at this question, ponder a bit more and in no more than 15 minutes write the answer to this question. The point is to have some sense of what is the main claim you want to make in response to the problem you have set yourself. This will allow you to have some idea of where this dissertation is going, because it is hard to plan a route without a destination.

Once you have done this you have the kernel of your introduction, that being a statement of the research topic and the basic question, and the kernel of your main claim or conclusion, that being the answer to the basic question which constitutes your research topic. Of course, all these may change but at least we have something which allows you to begin imagining and sketching the shape of the dissertation.

Mind map

We use the phrase 'mind map' with trepidation. Like 'free-writing', the exponents of mind mapping make extravagant claims for this technique. If you wish to explore mind mapping to the limits of its potential we suggest you read one of the several books introducing the technique and extolling the virtues of 'radiant thinking' (cf. Buzan 2006). The main benefit of 'mind mapping' is that it is closer to the messy nature of your project at this stage. It is a way of taking all the written and audio-visual stuff you have, all the ideas, quotes, images, incidents, bits of experience, research questions and so on, and beginning to make hierarchies and chart relationships.

Start by taking your newly rephrased research topic, boiling it down to one, two or three words and putting those words in a circle in the middle of a blank page. Now think about the main themes and issues that relate to your research question. Take five or ten minutes to do some free-writing to create a sentence or short paragraph describing these issues. Boil these related issues down to a few words, put these words in circles and place them on the page with a thick line to your main topic or question. You may find that these main themes and issues engender yet other lesser themes and issues which relate to them and so back to the main research question. So, again, do a bit of free-writing about these lesser themes and issues, make them into a few words in circles and place them on the page with lines connecting to other themes and issues. You may wish to begin charting various bits of evidence – incidents from your fieldnotes, images or bits of film, quotes by your informants, archival material or descriptions in published accounts by other scholars. Finally, you may wish to chart which secondary readings may specifically relate to a discussion of a given issue.

You cannot and should not be exhaustive here. Think of this as an organic entity, which will develop as you write. It is meant to be rough, unfinished and open to further transformation. The idea is to get you thinking about the shape of your dissertation: what relates to what, and what goes where.

The outline

Finally, you should transform this multidimensional, radiant mind-map into an outline for the dissertation as it will be written from beginning to end. If you have done some mind mapping beforehand then composing an outline should be straightforward. The description of the research topic and the formulation of the main research questions is the 'introduction'. Each of the main themes or issues you identified could become chapters, with the lesser themes and issues becoming sections within a chapter. In the conclusion you return to the research topic and the main research question and develop some kind of answer to that question drawing on the accumulation of claims and evidence that have been presented in the body of the dissertation.

Whether you are working from a mind map, or have engaged in what George Watson calls a 'stock-taking' process (1987: 34), you should wind up with a sequential list of chapter headings. Rowena Murray suggests you then write a couple of 'sentences on the contents of each chapter' (2006: 125). You may then wish to list the headings for each section of the chapter and write a couple of sentences describing what you will discuss under each of the headings. Finally, you should 'write an introductory paragraph for each chapter' (ibid.: 125). It is also important that you give a rough estimate for the word count of each chapter.

This outline will guide the writing of your dissertation. The degree to which it will do so is a matter of your own way of working, and finding a balance between spontaneous writing and having enough structure to ensure that your efforts are guided by some sense of how the various parts fit together as a whole.

Key points

- Return to your proposal, rewrite your research topic and identify your main research question(s).

- Use free-writing to switch off your 'inner editor' and get your ideas down on paper quickly.
- Use 'mind mapping' (or something like it) to sketch the relationship between your main research question(s), related issues, key readings and bits of evidence.
- From the mind map develop a linear dissertation outline.

Janet fashioned an outline. At first it looked a bit of a mess with lines and circles and more lines, but from this mess a story started to emerge. Right at the centre of her mind map she had the dead body made up to look whole and lifelike. Various questions came to her and she put them onto the mind map: 'why make the dead body lifelike?', 'what are the bodily aesthetics that inform the preparation of the corpse for viewing?' and 'how does the fact that the corpse is made beautiful inform or trouble anthropological understandings of the work of mourning?' She started to attach bits of her data and some of her reading to these questions. The anthropology of death seemed to come into the discussion of mourning as did the various conversations she had overheard at funerals. Her analysis of photographs would be at the centre of her discussion of the aesthetics of the corpse. The big question was the simplest one: 'why make the body lifelike and put it on display?' She would start with that. That could be described as emerging straight from her field-work. She could write it as a riddle of a sort: all this work behind the scenes to make the body appear as alive for a few hours or days and then have it buried. The answer? She was not sure yet but she figured her big point was that to understand death and mourning one needed to understand that deathliness or liveliness were aesthetic categories having to do with notions of the integrity of the body. So her introduction would pose the basic question in relation to her ethnography. Then she would have a chapter on the aesthetics of the corpse. Then she would have a chapter on mourning and memory. Then she would finish by making some kind of conclusion about the importance of understanding bodily aesthetics within our theorizations of mourning. Now she just had to write the darn thing.

Luck was everywhere for **John**, everywhere except in the academic writing on gambling. From his analysis his main question was already forming in his mind: 'why would gamblers hold to notions of good luck in spite of overwhelming evidence to the contrary?' He put this in the centre of his mind map. He had also decided that it would be a good move to frame this question by discussing the lack of writing about luck in much of the academic and policy literature concerning gambling in Britain. So he attached this discussion to his main question. Then what? Well, from his analysis he realized there was a lot of talk about luck. There was also a lot of talk about the 'science' of greyhound-racing. All the punters had elaborate systems for deciding which dog was most likely to win. The condition of the track, pedigree, the look of the dog before the race, all these came into consideration when choosing a winner. So he added 'science' and 'luck' as two separate categories related to his main question. During his reading he had come across the notion of 'magical thinking' in the social psychology literature, so maybe this could be a way to understand luck. But this seemed to assume it was something other than rational, when his analysis suggested luck and a rational appreciation of the odds and the likelihood of losing went hand-in-hand. So maybe this was his conclusion: 'that not only is luck important, but that luck cannot be understood as something opposite to, and defined by the absence of, rational thought'. A story was beginning to form. Finally, he decided that in his introduction he would address the literature on gambling and note the general absence of a discussion of luck. He would tell a few stories from his fieldwork to illustrate that luck is important to punters. On that basis he would state his main problematic. Then he would have a chapter exploring luck in detail. This would be richly ethnographic but would also relate to the literature on magical thinking. Then he would have a chapter on the 'science of greyhound-racing'. Then as a conclusion he would make the point that luck is not simply a delusional belief that sustains the gambling habit but works at the limits of a calculus of likelihood. Now he just had to write the darn thing.

Writing the darn thing

Now the time has come to write your dissertation. Before we turn to the question of how to compose an argument that is plausible and credible and relevant to anthropology, we should briefly consider how to organize your writing so as to finish the dissertation in good order and in good time.

First, you will need a schedule. You will have a due date for the dissertation. Take a couple of weeks off the date and make this into a deadline for the completion of a full draft of the dissertation. Why a couple of weeks? Once the draft is completed you will want to read through the draft, improving your argument, proof-reading and editing your text and perfecting its appearance on the page. You may also wish to give your supervisor a week or so to look over the draft and have some time to integrate her or his suggestions into the finished copy. Next, set a deadline for the completion of each chapter and add these dates to your dissertation outline. This is the schedule you will work to. There will be slips and adjustments. That is fine, so long as you do not rely on a miraculous final surge to get you past the post. A realistic schedule should keep you on track, assuming, of course, that you write steadily and with some focus.

Different people find different situations conducive to writing. It doesn't matter where and when you write. What matters is that you create the circumstances that allow you to write with concentration for a few hours at a stretch. When we say write for a few hours we mean 15 minutes, maybe half an hour, of actual writing. Then take five or ten minutes to ponder, flip through your notes, organize your thoughts, make a cup of tea. Then write for another 15 minutes and so on. The main thing is to work for a few hours and to not let the five or ten minutes of pondering extend to a half hour of checking emails and surfing the internet. This is your time to write. If you give it time the words will come.

Introducing the argument

This is the most straightforward bit of writing you will do. In introducing your argument you will be describing the central question your dissertation will be addressing, accounting for the significance of this question in reference to the existing literature pertaining to the issues you wish to address and giving some account for the methods by which you gained your understanding of the lives of others.

You will note that we have lumped together three things that are often treated separately: 'The Introduction', 'The Literature Review' and a discussion of methods and methodology. Whether you wish to present these as a part of your introduction or prefer them to be separated into two or three chapters is up to you. The tendency in social and cultural anthropology seems to be to enfold the review of the literature and a discussion of your research into the introduction, but there may be times when a more extended literature review and/or discussion of your research experience is warranted. In this case you should consider presenting these discussions as separate chapters.

The introduction

What does an introduction do? It introduces. To introduce someone or something is to provide orientation. Without a proper introduction your reader can become lost and confused. To orient themselves your reader needs some basic information.

First, they need to know what the dissertation is about. Before too many pages you should provide a clear statement of the topic of your dissertation and, not too long after that, present one, two, maybe three, basic research questions that pertain to this topic. If you have done as we have suggested and revised your proposal, done a bit of mind mapping and composed an outline then this should be straightforward. The main thing is to be precise in how you describe your topic. Remember that your reader is evaluating your dissertation. If it is evaluated properly then it will be evaluated within the terms you set yourself. You set these terms by stating your topic and research questions.

Second, they will need enough background information so they have some idea what you are talking about. In all likelihood your readers will not be so familiar with the peculiarities of the place(s) and people(s) you are writing about. So some basic orientation is required. We stress this is basic orientation. Much of the rich ethnographic detail concerning the place and people you have studied will be provided during the course of your discussion. Your introduction needs to provide just enough information so that they have some idea where they are and who they have found themselves amongst. Really what they need is facts. It may seem a bit old-fashioned, but a map never goes amiss. Some idea of the number and nature of the population is helpful. If it is pertinent to your discussion, some basic information concerning how people go about their everyday lives is also useful. A bit of scene-setting is a nice way to provide this orientation. Paint your reader a picture, whether this is a picture of a Bedouin village or a Brazilian institution for the ill and abandoned. This is why stories of arrival are so popular. It is not only the author who is arriving but through the author's account the reader also arrives and begins to find their way, as the author settles in, finds a place to stay and begins research.

Finally, your introduction should provide a basic outline of the chapters that constitute the body of the dissertation. These descriptions will likely be no more than a sentence or three and should come towards the close of your introduction. The main thing to remember is that this organization must make sense. There must be a reason for ordering the body of your dissertation in the way that you describe. You should communicate this sense to your reader in such a way that your approach to organizing your discussion seems a logical way of exploring a given topic and working your way towards an answer to the main question or problematic of your dissertation.

Reviewing the literature

In introducing your study you not only need to describe the topic of your dissertation and formulate some basic research questions; you also need to embed these research questions in a discussion of the literature pertinent to the topic. As with the review you produced for your research proposal, this is a matter of accounting for the relevance of your dissertation to broader traditions of anthropological scholarship, ethnographic study and philosophical speculation. What marks your dissertation as academic work is not only the quality of your research, analysis and argument; it is also the quality of your understanding of the traditions of scholarship within your discipline. These traditions of scholarship should be shown to clearly inform your own thinking concerning Balinese cockfights, Bedouin poetry, or whatever subject you have chosen to write about. Keep in mind that this is the introduction; you will continue to engage with and discuss the literature throughout your dissertation.

The question always is: how many books, chapters and articles do I need to discuss when writing a review of 'the literature'? There is, once again, no good answer. It is a particularly difficult question because for any anthropological topic the relevant literature is almost limitless; however, if you have followed the advice in the chapter on secondary research you will have cut this vast literary terrain down to size by adopting a systematic and structured approach to your reading. So to some extent you have already answered this question. That being said, writing is not the same as reading and note-taking. When writing a literature review there are a couple of points to keep in mind.

First, you are writing to secure the credibility of your dissertation as an academic piece of work. So your review should demonstrate you have engaged in a thoughtful and detailed manner with the literature relevant to your topic. What constitutes 'relevance' has been discussed in the chapter on secondary research in which we have emphasized the importance of constituting clear evaluative criteria for your literature searches that enable them to be at once *comprehensive* yet *specialized*. Your literature review does, however, need to be 'substantial', by which we mean that your engagement with the literature should evince some depth and breadth of reading.

Second, you need to remember that the point of discussing literature in an introduction is to formulate and refine your research questions. The purpose of this review is to critically evaluate what has been written on a subject in such a way that you can position your own study in relation to that body of writing. One way to think about it is as a process akin to drawing a map. What you want to do in writing a review of the literature is to sketch the scholarly terrain upon which you will be situating your own study. Like any good map that presages an adventure, there should be some blanks, or at least some areas which are poorly known or, to extend the metaphor, insufficiently charted. You then, in describing your topic, set yourself the mission of exploring this previously uncharted domain and so adding to our understanding of the human condition.

These blanks may be theoretically constituted. You may wish to demonstrate that a given phenomenon has been amply studied, but these studies have been of a particular theoretical disposition and therefore have ignored key issues or questions. Alternatively, these blanks may be ethnographically constituted, in that a given set of theoretical propositions has been well-developed in reference to one kind of situation, but have rarely been applied to the situation you are proposing to describe and understand.

Rarely are these gaps constituted by refuting the claims of other scholars. In general, social and cultural anthropology does not advance claims by over-turning previous truths and replacing them with newer, better truths. It works by enriching our previous accounts, by rendering them fuller and more nuanced. You should be wary of stating that the views of another academic are wrong or foolish. Such a statement will invariably read as simplistic, even presumptuous. It is more appropriate to provide a careful account of the significance of another's work in reference to your research topic, before suggesting some of the limitations of this work and how these limitations or contradictions have been addressed in other writings and potentially your own. This does not mean you cannot be critical, but this critique should proceed from a position of sympathetic and detailed understanding and then move to an account of some of the shortcomings of a given study or theoretical approach.

Describing your methods

Finally, in introducing your study you need to provide a transparent account of your research process and research methods. Again, this discussion may be presented as a separate chapter or it may be integrated into your introduction. If the local tradition is to have a 'research methods chapter', then you will have a research methods chapter. If there is no specific local directive then we would suggest that a research methods chapter is warranted only if the discussion of your methods is of particular methodological and theoretical interest concerning social scientific methods. In some cases your methods may actually be a significant part of what your dissertation is about.

In order to properly evaluate your claims your reader needs to know how it is that you came to know something about cockfighting in Bali, poetry amongst the Bedouin, and so on. This account needs to be detailed enough so that your reader has some idea of what you know and equally what you do not know. If this account is absent, or is so superficial it does not allow for an appreciation of the extent of your possible insight into the lives of others, then the credibility of claims that rest on the presumption of fieldwork may be deemed suspect.

What is required is then, to quote Abu-Lughod, 'an honest account of fieldwork', which is, she adds, 'essential for the evaluation of the facts and interpretation presented in the ethnographic report' (1999 [1986]: 9). Where anthropological studies are not based on ethnographic fieldwork the same holds true. If you have done your research in an archive or watching hours of documentary film, your readers will require an honest account of your research activities so they may have a clear understanding of how you went about coming to know the stuff you claim to know and are, by extension, in a position to critically evaluate these claims.

This 'honest account' should be a relatively simple description of how you got on, what you did and why you did it. Again, this does not mean that a description of your methods needs to be a dull enumeration of days spent in the field and number of people interviewed. Anthropological accounts of fieldwork often have a vivid intimacy that is lacking in descriptions of research methods in more positivistically oriented social sciences. There is a good reason for this. Anthropological knowledge is predicated on the assumption of a familiarity with the lives of others. By describing your fieldwork experience as an *experience*, that is, as something lived through in the unfolding encounter with other people and other places, you suggest this quality of familiarity which renders your account of the lives of others credible.

Such vivid descriptions of the experience of fieldwork should not, however, be considered to be a replacement for a clear account of the research process. Be careful to avoid the trap of assuming that because you went to a place and lived there for a while you have studied 'a culture' or 'a society'. Cultures and societies, if they exist at all, are big and complex. In reality what you did was meet some people, ask some questions, and read some documents or books. From this experience you may choose to generate a more general description of 'a culture' and 'a society', but you did not meet with or ask questions to such an entity. To judge the credibility of these generalizations, and other claims that you will be making, your reader needs to have some *specific* idea of who you met with, how you got on, what questions you asked, or what documents and books you read.

So now you have introduced your study. Your reader should have a clear understanding of what your dissertation is about, what big questions you will be discussing and may be trying to resolve, and some sense of how your project is informed by anthropological scholarship. They should know something of how you went about your research and came to know something of the lives of others to the extent that you can speak with some credibility about these lives. What now? Now you need to fashion an argument.

Key points

- Your introduction should describe the main topic of your dissertation, provide background information and outline the organization of your discussion.
- Embed your topic within a critical review of the literature and refine your main research problematic or issue.
- Provide a transparent, 'honest account' of your research process and methods, in enough detail for your reader to make a reasonable judgement about the credibility of your claims based on your research.
- Do not be afraid to make this account vivid and personal, but remember your reader needs the facts as well!

Janet had written her introduction. She had eased into things by writing of her fieldwork, describing how she had come to work in the funeral parlour, the escalating drug- and gang-related violence, the new vernacular embalmers, and how she got on with the staff and followed them as they attended funerals. She described how the embalmers worked to make the corpse of a road-traffic victim into someone his family would want to see. At the end they looked at their handiwork, 'beautiful,' they said, 'what a handsome man.' After a couple of pages she moved from this anecdote to her main question: 'why make a corpse beautiful?' With the basic problem clearly stated she elaborated this question with reference to the literature. She brought in some writing about the work of undertakers elsewhere and noted that making the body beautiful and lifelike was a recurrent feature of this work. She addressed the literature on funerary customs and noted that, although there was a lot of discussion of the preparation of the corpse, there was no discussion of aesthetics. This allowed her to write a more refined and theoretically articulate version of her main research question: 'how could an appreciation of ideas of beauty and the beautiful body inform our understanding of funerary rituals and the work of mourning?' She then wrote that her discussion of this problem would be in two parts, the first about the aesthetics of the dead body and the second about mourning and the lifelike corpse. Her argument had begun.

John began his introduction by addressing the literature on 'problem' gambling. He very briefly reviewed this literature and suggested that if luck was discussed at all it was described as a delusional belief that was a feature of the 'psychopathology of problem gambling'. Perhaps because of this assumption, John argued, there had been very few studies of gambling which focused on luck and on that basis truly understood how gamblers thought of and experienced 'luck'. With this brief literature review in place John was ready to define the topic of his dissertation. His dissertation was about luck and gambling. 'In exploring the topic of luck and gambling' he declared that he was 'going to explore the rationality of luck'. 'I will argue,' he wrote, 'that luck is not a delusional belief but a feature of a rational calculus of probability that nonetheless leads punters to keep betting even in the knowledge they are more likely to lose than win.' With his main topic defined John moved on to describe his case study. He explained why he chose to study greyhound-racing, how he became familiar with the subtleties of betting and befriended some of the regulars at the track. In so doing he not only gave an account of his fieldwork, but made sure his reader knew enough about greyhound-racing to make sense of the rest of his argument. Now to write the rest.

Fashioning the argument

But how exactly does one go about composing this argument that will constitute the substance (and by that we mean most of the words) of your dissertation? The answer is elusive. It is particularly elusive in anthropology because anthropologists have, to some extent, dispensed with the logic of presentation that informs academic writing in more positivistically inclined social sciences. In this tradition, a report often takes the form of an introduction, followed by a literature review, then an account of the study and the methodology employed, followed by a description of the results of the study (which is, in effect, the results of the data analysis, the raw data rarely being presented in full) and finally a discussion of the results that suggests their relevance to the original research question and to broader theoretical issues that have been elaborated within the traditions of scholarship within which the research question is articulated (cf. Robson 2002: 140–42).

Anthropologists have retained some of these habits. There is often an introduction which either includes, or is followed by, a brief description of the research methods and some discussion of the more general literature pertinent to the main research questions. Once we are beyond the introduction, however, it can seem like a bit of a free-for-all. Discussions of the literature, presentations of findings, quotes and anecdotes, theoretical propositions and philosophical speculation all seem to be jumbled up together. The distinction between data, findings and the interpretation of findings is, therefore, more muddled and less clear-cut in anthropological writings. Accordingly, anthropological studies can vary considerably in their form of argumentation and presentation.

Claims and evidence

Despite these differences, there are some broad similarities in the ways in which anthropologists write their arguments. Fundamentally, anthropologists, as social scientists, advance various claims concerning the whys and wherefores of human existence, claims which are at once specific to the circumstances of the study and yet aspire to speak to issues that are greater than these circumstances. These claims are all supported by evidence. This evidence is, directly or indirectly, evidence concerning the lives of real people. A good piece of anthropological writing is, as we suggested earlier, one that advances claims that are credible and plausible, in that they are sustained by the evidence of your own research or by the published work of others whose findings are deemed credible and plausible by the academic community.

Of course, these observations are hardly novel. In particular, our focus on the claims and evidence, and the plausibility and relevance of ethnographic accounts is borrowed from Martin Hammersley's *Reading Ethnographic Research* (1998) and Kate Turabian's *Manual for Writers of Research Papers, Theses and Dissertations* (2007). For Turabian, a claim is your thesis. It is 'the centre of your argument' and 'the point of your report' (2007: 51). Such claims, by their very nature, require evidence to render them plausible. Hammersely makes a similar point. In so doing he makes a distinction that is useful when thinking about writing ethnographic research. This is a distinction between 'main claims' and 'evidentiary claims'.

Main claims are the basic propositions and central points that constitute the fundamental findings of your research. Evidentiary claims are the evidence that the writer uses to support the main claims and, by so doing, render them plausible. It is worth noting that Hammersely writes of 'evidentiary claims', rather than evidence. The difference is subtle yet important. We commonly think of ourselves as presenting evidence, which is the irreducible stuff of reality which constitutes the material from which we fashion our main claims. When writing up, however, what we present is rarely the irreducible stuff of reality; it is, rather, a representation of that reality that claims to be true and faithful to that reality. As such, as Hammersley makes clear, these claims can be judged according to their plausibility and, in particular, their credibility in much the same way as one would judge the plausibility and credibility of bigger, wider, more abstract claims.

So we fashion our argument of main claims, whose plausibility is secured by evidentiary claims, which in turn may require some more evidence to secure their plausibility and credibility. This relationship between main claims and evidentiary claims is fundamental to the fashioning of an anthropological argument, as is securing the credibility of evidentiary claims with a clear account of their provenance. This seems sensible in theory. When it comes to practicalities of writing a dissertation, however, there are two bothersome questions concerning the relationship between claims and evidence.

The first question is: how much evidence do you need to present in support of your main claims? The answer is 'enough' that your main claims will be read as plausible. This does not mean that you will have 'proved' your main claim to be true beyond any shadow of doubt. Anthropology is, at best, an inexact science and does not really deal in absolute truth. It does, however, deal in provisional, plausible truths which are secured by the quality of the argument and the evidence presented in support of your proposition.

Moreover, the nature of your evidence should be roughly proportionate to the nature of your claim. What do we mean by this? Well think of it from the point of view of a reader of academic work. Say you pick up a paper about the Balinese Cockfight written by Clifford Geertz. In it he makes a whole bunch of claims. One of them is that there exists a 'deep psychological identification of Balinese men with their cocks' (1973: 60). Now, if you are reading critically you will think to yourself: 'Really? How do you know this to be so?' So he tells you how he knows. His Balinese landlord once said to Geertz 'I'm cock crazy'. Is this enough? It may be enough to support the claim that Geertz's landlord is into cockfighting, but Geertz is not saying this. He is saying Balinese men in general closely identify with fighting cocks. So we need more evidentiary claims. And we get them. We are told in some detail about how Balinese men attend to their birds with lavish care and affection (ibid.: 61). We are told that in everyday talk and poetry men are often likened to cocks, in their pride, their heroism, or even in their failings, as a pompous man is likened 'to a tailless cock who struts about as though he had a large, spectacular one', or a stingy man is 'compared to a cock which, held by the tail, leaps at another without in fact engaging him' (ibid.: 60). All of this does not mean you, the reader, have to agree with Geertz's main claim, but you will likely concede that it is a plausible assertion given the evidence he presents.

This brings us to the second question: if we talk of 'evidentiary claims' rather than 'evidence' then when can we decide that the claims we are making can be considered self-evident and we can stop providing more evidence to support our evidentiary claims? Again, this is a tricky question. Basically, it is a matter of provenance. If an evidentiary claim is to be read as credible the reader must feel confident that it comes from a credible source.

Generally speaking, there are two types of credible source. The first is your own field research. Your own empirical ethnographic data gives a lot of licence to you as the anthropologist to write authoritatively of the lives of others. For example, in 'Notes on the Balinese Cockfight' Geertz makes the following evidentiary claim:

> Whenever you see a group of Balinese men squatting idly in the council shed or along the road in their hips down, shoulders forward, knees up fashion, half or more of them will have a rooster in his hands, holding it between his thighs, bouncing it gently up and down to strengthen its legs, ruffling its feathers with abstract sensuality, pushing it out against a neighbour's rooster to rouse its spirit, withdrawing it toward his loins to calm it again.
>
> (Geertz 1973: 459)

Geertz, as he assures us in the preamble of his article, lived in a Balinese village. He went to cockfights and attended closely to talk of fighting cocks. So when he presents evidence such as this we find it credible because we believe that he has actually witnessed Balinese men crouching with their roosters held lovingly between their knees.

The other source of credible evidence is the published works of reputable scholars. Why? The simple answer is because we can trust them and trust that the evidentiary claims they make are credible. The more complex answer is that works published by the academic community have been subjected to rigorous scrutiny by specialists in the field (Hammersely 1998: 68–70). This is why evidentiary claims made in books and journal articles written by professional academics and published by academic publishers are much more likely to be regarded as plausible and credible than material published on Wikipedia. Of course, the reality of academic work does not always live up to these ideals of rigour and scrutiny, but nonetheless evidentiary claims are more likely to be regarded as credible if they are taken from credible sources.

This is why properly citing your sources of information is so crucial. If the credibility of evidentiary claims rest on their provenance then your reader must know where this information is coming from. The conventions of citation and referencing are not just a matter of adhering to the 'rules' of academic writing; the proper attribution of sources is critical to establishing the credibility of your claims. There is much guidance as to various approaches to citing sources and listing those references. Your first stop should, again, be any specific directions published by your institution. Some universities have a preferred format or style when it comes to citing sources and composing bibliographies and reference lists. Others are happy with any approach, so long as it adheres to proper academic conventions and is consistent. In the latter case, it is a good idea to consult one of several good style manuals available.

The first step to writing an argument is, therefore, to link your main claim to evidentiary claims and to ensure that these evidentiary claims are credible by reference to your own research or the work of others. Now, how do we weave this all together into some kind of argument?

Zooming in and zooming out

We would argue that, by and large, anthropologists weave together their arguments by shifting perspectives. Sometimes we write of things up close. We describe, as well as words will allow, some real event. We speak of real, specific people, doing and saying real and specific things. At other times we write of things from a distance, speaking of what people do in general, even theoretical, terms. The trick is how we accomplish this shift of perspective in writing.

A lovely example is Keith Basso's famous essay 'Stalking with Stories' (1996), in which he follows the words of his Apache informants to suggest an interpretation of the historical tales they tell. A few pages in and we are driving in the company of Basso. He stops his jeep at the camp of an old Apache man named Nick Thompson. Nick is smoking a mentholated cigarette and relaxing in his chair outside his cabin, with a mug of coffee and a copy of the *National Enquirer* in easy reach (1996: 24). After a minute or two of amiable silence Nick enquires as to the purpose of Basso's visit. Basso tells him that he is 'puzzled by certain statements the Apache have made about the country' and 'anxious to know how to interpret them' (ibid.: 24). 'Learn the names', says Nick, 'start with the names' (ibid.). For ten weeks Nick teaches the anthropologist place names and the anthropologist, true to his trade, writes them onto a map. Shortly before Basso is set to leave at the close of the summer, Nick asks to see these maps. 'He,' writes Basso, 'is not impressed. "White men need paper maps", he observes, "we have maps in our minds"' (ibid.: 25).

This is not a description of Apache culture or society. This is a description of Keith Basso meeting Nick Thompson and learning about place names. Nick Thompson is not a common denominator person (Marcus and Cushman 1982: 32–33), or what Jonathan Spencer caustically labelled *homo ethnographicus* (1989: 153). He is Nick Thompson, who cuts his white hair short, smokes menthol cigarettes and reads the *National Enquirer*. When he tells us that we must understand place names to understand Apache stories he is not speaking as a typical Apache, he is speaking as himself, in his own words (or so it seems), although these words do indeed lead us to more general and profound insights into Apache culture.

Your dissertation, however, cannot be composed simply of a series of descriptions of incidents and quotes from various informants. You also need to take a step back and write accounts of what people tend to do, say, think and feel as a group. Basso does just that. He tells the story of Nick Thompson and the mapping of place names, then a few pages later he takes a step back and suggests that it is not just Nick Thompson who is interested in place names, it is Apaches in general. 'Apaches,' he asserts, 'enjoy using them' (the 'them' being place names). Then he moves back in close and writes of a time he was stringing barbed wire with a couple of Apache cowboys, one of whom takes to muttering place names softly under his breath as he works. When the anthropologist asks him why he is doing this, the cowboy replies that he likes to, and that he rides 'that way in my mind' (1996: 27). Then Basso takes a step back again and tell us that 'on dozens of other occasions when I have been working or travelling with Apaches, they have taken satisfaction in pointing out particular locations and pronouncing their names' (ibid.).

One way of thinking about this shifting of perspectives is in terms of 'zooming in' and 'zooming out'. In other words you 'zoom in' on specific events or specific things people did and said and 'zoom out' to more generalized descriptions of relationships and regularities and, on that basis, to more theoretical and even philosophical discussions. What you are doing is forging associations. This is in part a matter of forging associations between things at the same level, as Keith Basso does when relating Nick Thompson's enigmatic talk about the importance of place names to a cowboy mumbling names under his breath as he strings barbed wire. More importantly, this is a matter of forging associations between the various levels of your discussion. You need to account for how the stringing of barbed wire indicates something more general about the significance of place names amongst the Apache which in turn indicates something even more general about the relationship of indigenous peoples to the land.

In 'zooming in' and 'zooming out' you are constituting the significance of the specific doings and sayings that you are describing by situating them within broader and more theoretically constituted discussions. As with everything we have said in this chapter, it is important to remember that this process of 'zooming in' and 'zooming out' is not just a way of imagining research or analyzing your findings. It is a way of composing your argument in such a way that your main claims will be read as emerging from and supported by your evidence. The key to this composition is the way you forge associations in writing. You do this by referring back and forward. You refer back to explain how what you are about to write leads on from what you have already written. Alternatively, you refer forward from what you have just written to suggest how you will proceed.

It is in this process of 'zooming in' and 'zooming out' that you relate your main claims to your evidentiary claims and compose an argument that weaves together rich and detailed descriptions of everyday life, as it was revealed to you in your fieldwork and as you have learned of it through written sources, more general accounts of culture and society, and theoretical arguments concerning the nature of human relationships. In this composition you constitute rich and detailed descriptions, more general accounts and theoretical arguments. More importantly, you constitute the associations between these various elements. By constituting these webs of associations you move the argument forward towards its conclusion by introducing problems and questions and working through the dense detail of lived existence towards some resolution of these problems or answers to these questions.

For more detail about 'zooming in' and 'zooming out' as well as how anthropologists compose relationships between various claims and bits of evidence (from your fieldwork, archival or secondary research), take a look at my discussion of Keith Basso's 'Stalking with Stories' (1996) and Matei Candea's (2010) article about falling in love with Carlos the meerkat on the companion website.

Key points

- You write a plausible and credible argument by composing associations between 'evidentiary claims' and more theoretical or general statements.
- You compose these associations by changing scale, or 'zooming in' on small details and then 'zooming out' to more general statements that describe the significance of these small details in theoretical terms.
- The key to this is passages of writing that 'look back' and 'look forward', thereby linking the writing that has come before with the writing that will come after.

Concluding the argument

Your conclusion is often the shortest section of your dissertation. Normally, you should not present any new ideas or lines of argument. Your conclusion should be about drawing these lines together to compose a final statement that will close the line of enquiry you have opened in your introduction. Of course, this is easier said than done. By now you will have covered a lot of ground, raised a lot of issues, and closing this can be difficult. This is all the more so because anthropology is, as we have said, not a particularly positivistic discipline and rarely will your analysis be oriented towards testing a hypothesis. Your conclusions are, therefore, likely to be somewhat more vague and suggestive and so harder to summarize briefly and neatly.

Your conclusion should basically do two related things: 1) It should summarize the argument that constituted the main body of your dissertation, and 2) It should return to your introduction and consider how this argument relates and enhances our understanding of the main research questions that you described as being the focus for your study. It may be too much to hope that these questions will be 'answered' (often there are no answers), but you should account for how your study has enriched our understanding of the area under study. Often this is a matter of 'zooming out' once more to address some fundamental theoretical problem or issue within the literature. Your conclusion should close the circle you started by the theoretical problem you described in your introduction. Of course, no circle is ever closed and even in returning to the question and summarizing your answer, you may also wish to suggest new questions, possibilities for further studies and ways that the circle of enquiry can be opened again.

You should be familiar by now with the stylistic conventions of anthropology and the preferences of your own institution when it comes to grammar, punctuation and presentation. For our own advice on writing style and some interesting stuff on unconventional experiments in writing culture, take a look at our companion website.

Staying sane, getting help, getting finished

It had all started so well for **Janet**. Her introduction was so clearly imagined and well outlined that she wrote it in a few days. The chapter on the aesthetics of the body proved almost a pleasure to write as well. She worked through her analysis of her photographs, 'zooming in' on specific details, contextualizing these within narratives rewritten from her fieldnotes, and then 'zooming out' through more theoretical works to develop her argument concerning the curious beauty of the corpse. Through this time she met with her supervisor, who glanced over what she had written so far and seemed content with her progress. Then she came to the chapter on mourning and memory. She started writing and then got lost. It seemed too complex. She had plenty of material from her research. She also had plenty of notes from her reading. She had a rough outline as well, but when she started writing, the argument just seemed to go nowhere. She started to dread writing. She stopped for some days citing the pressures of other academic work. It proved hard to start again. Days passed and her anxiety built. Curiously, the more anxious she became the harder it seemed to concentrate on writing. She had a meeting with her supervisor. Before the meeting he had read through her chapter, a bit more carefully this time. He seemed remarkably positive about what she had written. It seemed to him that she had been suggesting that the final viewing of the corpse was to create a final 'image' of the person to be remembered. It was not unlike her photographs. He pointed her to a few articles on photography and memory. He also told her he wanted a finished draft of the chapter in a week. She had a quick look at the articles and things seemed to connect. She started writing. The draft took ten days but she emailed it to her supervisor. Then the conclusion. Then two weeks of proof-reading and making changes and finally she was done.

John was progressing nicely. The introduction was done. He had written his chapter on luck, working mostly through his own research material and using his critical engagement with the notion of magical thinking as a way of 'zooming out' to constitute the theoretical significance of his findings. He met regularly with his supervisor. She suggested that he look to the anthropological literature on magic, particularly in Africa, as a possible area in which 'magical thinking' was treated as a rational system. Everything was going fine until his older brother was in a biking accident. It was serious, very serious. John's family was thrown into turmoil. John couldn't think straight. He went home to be with his family for a week and then came back, but he was not the same. If he sat down to work he felt he was ignoring his brother. How could he work at a time like this? He went to see his supervisor. She suggested that, given the circumstances, an extension was possible. John's brother remained in hospital, still in a critical condition for two weeks. John finally asked for a month's extension. His friends were great too. Several offered to help in any way they could. One was known to be scrupulous when it came to grammar, spelling and punctuation. With two weeks to go, John gave her a copy of his complete draft and a week later it came back electronically with all errors and changes marked in red. His brother improved and John submitted his dissertation the day before his extended deadline.

Finishing a substantial piece of writing is tough. It is not tough all the time. Sometimes the words will be flowing, your argument will be clear in your mind and you will be feeling good and happy with the dissertation writing. At other times, however, the words will not come, your thoughts will be confused and jumbled and you may well feel despondent, if not downright despairing of ever finishing anything like an adequate piece of writing. So how do you get through this?

There is, as with all of this, no magical piece of advice that will make everything easy and ok. Everyone is different and everyone deals with the pressures of delivering a substantial piece of academic writing to a deadline in different ways. Here, however, are a few suggestions.

Be realistic

This is an undergraduate dissertation to be submitted in the fulfillment of the requirements of your degree. You need to present an argument that is focused on a clearly defined topic. The main claims of this argument need to be made plausible and credible by reference to the evidence and be relevant to some key issues and questions that are embedded within anthropological traditions of scholarship. This argument needs to be presented clearly and pleasingly so that your reader can appreciate the points you are making. You need to do this within a set word limit and deliver this document by a set deadline. That is it. Your dissertation is unlikely to set the academic world alight. You do not need to be better than any of your peers. You have a job to do and that job is to write a good dissertation with only as much pain and fuss as is required of such an endeavour.

Keep writing

When the words come slowly it is easy to become despondent and drift away from the work of writing. Do not do this. By all means take a break. Go for a walk. Have a coffee with friends. But then get back at it. If you keep working away the words will come. You may not feel happy with them. You may think you are writing nonsense, but keep writing. Do not second-guess yourself after every sentence and paragraph. Resist the temptation to delete everything and start again. You can only judge the quality of your writing from a slight distance. You will need to read and revise, but other than minor revisions and corrections do not do so 'on the fly'. Finish a section or a chapter, then take a break, then read it through and make some revisions to improve the flow and clarity of your argument. Similarly, if you think you have lost the thread of your argument or have gone off on some crazy tangent do not panic. Finish your section or chapter. Stop, re-read it. Chances are a little tweaking and cutting and pasting may sort things out.

Do not suffer in silence

In general do what you can to make writing a dissertation a social process. Talk about your work with others. Seek sympathy, care and support from those in your life who will offer you sympathy, care and support. The important thing is not to hide away with your work and your anxieties about your work. This is particularly true if, for whatever reason, you find you are truly struggling with writing a dissertation. This may be because you are experiencing personal difficulties which distract you from this work. This may also be because you are finding writing a clear and coherent anthropological argument peculiarly difficult and anxiety provoking. Whatever the situation, however, the main thing is not to suffer in silence. If you are in difficulty speak to people about your difficulties and seek their help, support and guidance. There is no shame in struggling. We have all struggled. **If you are in difficulties, and it seems like these difficulties threaten to compromise the successful and timely completion of your dissertation, then you *must* tell your supervisor and any who are involved with directing or overseeing your studies.** This is set in bold because it is very important. It may not always seem like it, but your lecturers, tutors and supervisor all want you to do well. If you are in difficulties and they can help, then they will. But you must speak to them about your situation and do so as soon as you become aware that you are in difficulty. If you wait to the last days and hours before submission then the help they can offer is much more limited.

Work with your supervisor

Almost all universities will assign you a supervisor who will help to guide you through the process of researching and writing a dissertation. What do supervisors do? Well, they supervise. This usually consists of semi-regular meetings. During these meetings you will likely discuss your progress, what you have written so far and where your writing is going, and on that basis agree to some timetables for your work. Your supervisor may request that you send them chapters as they are completed and may provide feedback concerning what you have written. Your supervisor may well help with readings and, being an academic anthropologist, should be able to help suggest how best to situate your argument within broader traditions of anthropological writing. It is possible that your supervisor may read through an entire draft of your dissertation and provide detailed corrections. But this does not happen with all supervisors at all institutions. More than anything else your supervisor is there as someone with whom you can talk through ideas, lines of argument, difficulties, points of confusion and so on. They will not have all the answers but they should be able to help you think and write.

You have every right to expect good and helpful supervision. There must, however, be limits to these expectations. Your supervisor is not there to help you with every sentence and paragraph. This is your dissertation, your research, your analysis, and your argument which will be made in your words and for the most you will need to get on with it. Nor is the supervisor there as a counsellor or confessor. You *must* go to your supervisor if you are experiencing difficulties that may inhibit you from writing a good dissertation in good time. They are there to support you with the academic aspects of these difficulties and it is crucial that you seek their support in this capacity. They are not necessarily there to support you with the emotional, psychological or social aspects of these difficulties. They should be sympathetic and human, but if you find yourself in real distress then, as well as working with your supervisor to keep your work on track, you should also seek help and support elsewhere.

Your university will likely have guidance as to what constitutes the minimum responsibilities of a supervisor. You would do well to familiarize yourself with this guidance. If it seems that you are not receiving adequate supervision as it is defined by this guidance then you would do well to raise this issue with the director of your programme and perhaps seek an alternate supervisor. Otherwise, you should make use of your supervisor in whatever way suits you best and best supports the successful completion of your dissertation.

The best thing is to reach clear agreements with your supervisor about what they will do for you (and in turn what you will do for them). Then you should both, as much as possible, stick to these agreements. If you agree to get a chapter to them by Friday next week then you should send them a chapter by Friday next week. If you cannot do so then get in touch to tell them why and when they can expect the chapter. If, in turn, they agree that they will have the chapter returned to you with comments a few days after they receive it then you should expect this to be done or, if it is not done, then at least to hear something from them. If you agree to a meeting you should show up on time and so, for that matter, should your supervisor. Of course, we all fail to meet our agreements sometimes, supervisors and students alike. The main thing is to keep communicating, try one's best to stick to what has been agreed, and if things go wrong and your plans go awry then be open and honest and make some revised plans. Finally, you should be polite and considerate and you should have every expectation to be treated with politeness and consideration.

Work with others

Your supervisor cannot and should not be your only source of help and support through the process of writing your dissertation. There are plenty of ways other people can help.

It may be that you would wish to talk over your ideas with other lecturers or tutors who have some expertise peculiar to your area of research. They are not your supervisor and have no requirement to agree to take the time to meet and talk over ideas, but most academics are intellectually generous and if approached are happy to talk things over. The main thing to remember is to tell your supervisor if you are seeking some advice and inspiration from other scholars. It can be a frustrating experience for both you and your supervisor if you are given conflicting advice on how to develop your ideas and write your dissertation.

When it comes to proof-reading for spelling and grammar, friends and family can be a great help. Be sure to give whoever is proof-reading your work (and this includes yourself) enough time to do it. If you are in dire straights, or you have particular problems with your prose and writing proper, grammatically correct English, then there are professional proof-reading services available. Some may be offered for free through your university. Otherwise it is easy to find someone who will do it for money (many provide their services over the internet). If you do go down that route then shop around, and make sure they are a credible and well-reviewed service.

Seek support if you need it

Finally, if you find yourself getting particularly distressed during the process of writing your dissertation or are coping with other situations in your life that are causing you considerable worry and anxiety, you may wish to seek the support of counselling services. These likely will be available through your university. The main thing, as we stressed earlier, is not to suffer in silence. Academic staff should be sympathetic and helpful when it comes to academic matters, but they are not best placed and also not qualified to deal with emotional distress. Again, there is no shame in needing help of all kinds through this process and in the unlikely event that you feel yourself unable to cope then you should not hesitate to get the right kind of help from the right kind of people.

Keep things in proportion. A dissertation is a dissertation. It is important, but it is not everything and the whole world. Writing up your research can be intellectually absorbing and exciting. There is real satisfaction to be found in composing your own ideas from research that you have done. Writing a dissertation can also be hard and stressful. That is ok. A bit of hardship and stress is to be expected. It may even be a good thing (if we ran away from stress and hardship we would never do anything). But it is a good thing only if you are coping with it and not neglecting yourself and others. So above all else attend to your well-being. Attend to the well-being of those close to you. And enjoy life!

References

Abu-Lughod, Lila. 1999 (1986). *Veiled Sentiments: Honour and Poetry in a Bedouin Society*. Berkeley: University of California Press.

Basso, Keith. 1996. 'Stalking with Stories'. In K. Basso, *Wisdom Sits in Places: Landscape and Language amongst Western Apache*. Albuquerque, NM: University of New Mexico Press, pp. 37–70.

Biehl, João. 2005. *Vita: Life in a Zone of Abandonment*. Berkeley: University of California Press.

Boon, James. 1982. *Other Tribes, Other Scribes: Symbolic Anthropology in the Comparative Study of Cultures, Histories, Religions and Texts*. Cambridge: Cambridge University Press.

Buzan, Tony. 2006. *The Mind Map Book*. Harlow, Essex: BBC Active.

Candea, Matei. 2010. 'I Fell in Love with Carlos the Meerkat: Engagement and Detachment in Human–Animal Relations', *American Ethnologist*, 37(2): 241–58.

Clifford, James and George E. Marcus (eds). 1986. *Writing Culture: The Poetics and Politics of Ethnography*. Berkeley: University of California Press.

Ellen, Roy. F. 1984. *Ethnographic Research: A Guide to General Conduct*. London: Academic Press.

Gay y Blasco, Paloma and Huon Wardle. 2007. *How to Read Ethnography*. London: Routledge.

Geertz, Clifford. 1973. 'Deep Play: Notes on the Balinese Cockfight'. In C. Geertz, *The Interpretation of Cultures: Selected Essays by Clifford Geertz*. New York: Basic Books, pp. 411–53.

Hammersley, Martyn. 1998. *Reading Ethnographic Research: A Critical Guide*. 2nd edition. Harlow, Essex: Longman Books.

Marcus, George E. and Dick Cushman. 1982. 'Ethnographies as Texts', *Annual Review of Anthropology*, 11: 25–69.

Murray, Rowena. 2006. *How to Write a Thesis*. 2nd edition. Maidenhead: Open University Press.

Robson, Colin. 2002. *Real World Research: A Source for Social-scientists and Practitioner Researchers*. Oxford: Blackwell.

Spencer, Jonathan. 1989. 'Anthropology as a Kind of Writing', *Man*, new series, 24(1): 145–64.

Turabian, Kate. 2007. *A Manual for Writers of Research Papers, Theses and Dissertations: Chicago Style for Students and Researchers*. 7th edition. Chicago: University of Chicago Press.

Watson, George. 1987. *Writing a Thesis: A Guide to Long Essays and Dissertations*. London: Longman.

Conclusion

After the dissertation

Natalie Konopinski

Once you have submitted your dissertation you may just want to celebrate, sit back and relax for a week or two. But it might also be a good time to start planning some follow-up activities and thinking about what you have learned through the research process. The research and main writing project may be over, but the value of the whole experience far exceeds the immediate academic product. In short, your research is much more than the dissertation. You may, for example, want to write shorter versions of some of the key themes or chapters, perhaps for a blog, student journal, or popular publication. If an organization gave you help, access or placement opportunities you ought perhaps to send them a brief report. Since the whole process will have greatly increased your capabilities as an independent researcher, you could note down some of the key lessons you have learned or capacities you have developed, with a view to letting others (future employers or research grant-givers, for example) know about your skills and experience.

Dissemination: sharing and publishing your research

There are several ways in which you can share your research findings with a wider academic or public audience.

Reports and presentations

You may wish, or have already committed, to provide feedback to your research participants. Particularly if you conducted research or fieldwork in organizational or institutional settings, this can be a good way to thank the people who contributed to your work. If this is the case you may want to revise your dissertation into a short report describing your main analysis and conclusions. It is worth bearing in mind that participants may be interested, disinterested and even uninterested in the final written product. While few people are likely to want to read the entire dissertation, many will be interested in the parts that relate to them, or their organization, and any major analytical arguments you have made. A research report gives interlocutors or participants a chance to engage with and critique your academic work, and can provide you with additional insights and opinions on your material.

If your research has original or practical social policy implications to do with health, education or migration, for example, you could tailor a policy brief for the relevant local government department or independent interest group. If you have not already made contact with a suitable person or organization during the research process, it could be useful to do so. For example, you could email a communications officer or researcher at a local or national government department to discuss your research with them ahead of time, find out what issues they are interested in hearing more about, and tailor your report accordingly.

If you conducted research with members of a particular community, club, social or political group of some sort, you may want to give a report in the form of a short presentation. If you do give a presentation, consider your audience and be aware that you may be stepping into sensitive territory (Walliman 2005: 261). As Nicholas Walliman suggests, it may be worth making sure the members or leaders of the group know about the content of your talk and are cognizant of your main arguments beforehand (ibid.).

If you decide to share your research, and however you choose to do so, remember that the dissertation and any report based on it are a product of your own research experience, interpretation and analysis; your participants will form their own opinions and perspectives on your work.

Conference papers, posters and visual presentations

Writing an academic conference paper based on particular themes or chapters from your dissertation and giving a short presentation on this can be an excellent way to share your research with your peers and the wider academic community. The same applies if your research outputs are predominantly visual, such as anthropological film and photography. Your university department should have information about student-specific conferences or the student sections of academic conferences. Equally, you may wish to submit a paper to an interdisciplinary conference or one based on a geographic or academic area related to your particular project. If you have produced a film as part of your research outputs you could take a look at the student sections of any ethnographic film festivals or conferences. Many conferences also have space for student photo essays or student posters on which you present information about your research project. It is worth trying to imagine how an academic audience unfamiliar, or less familiar, with the subject than you are will understand it and what they will find stimulating.

Exhibitions and film screenings

If your research outputs include significant visual products, a photography exhibition or film screening, for example, may be a good way to provide feedback to research participants or to reach a broader public audience. Your university may have a suitable space for this, or you might want to check out the gallery or art spaces in your town, city or local community.

Journal articles

There are an increasing number of exciting outlets for undergraduate and M.Sc. level students in student-run journals and e-journals. Writing an academic article will enable you to enter dialogue with fellow students and faculty, experience the peer review process and receive critical feedback on your work. Journals provide a medium for the exchange of ideas and knowledge and also offer the opportunity to establish new connections with people whose research interests match your own. It will also make an impressive addition to your CV, particularly if you wish to pursue a postgraduate degree or Ph.D. You will probably need to tackle the transition from dissertation to academic publication on your own, however. A supervisor's job does not extend beyond the dissertation, although she or he may be willing to read a draft and offer initial comments to help you on your way.

Some useful resources:

The Council on Undergraduate Research (US) lists a number of undergraduate research journals at http://www.cur.org/resources/students/undergraduate_journals

Hartley, James. 2008. *Academic Writing and Publishing: A Practical Handbook.* London and New York: Routledge.

Reinvention: An International Journal of Undergraduate Research is produced and edited by students and academic staff at the University of Warwick (UK) and Monash University (Australia). The journal is available to read online and offers useful tips for first-time article writers: http://www2.warwick.ac.uk/fac/cross_fac/iatl/ejournal

Box 9.1

A selection of journals edited by and for anthropology students

Argot (Johns Hopkins University)
http://anthropology.jhu.edu/argot/index.html

Ethnographic Encounters (University of St Andrews)
http://ojs.st-andrews.ac.uk/index.php/SAEE

Imponderabilia: The International Student Anthropology Journal (Cambridge University)
http://imponderabilia.socanth.cam.ac.uk

Journal of Undergraduate Anthropology (Binghampton University)
http://anthrojournal.binghampton.edu

University of California Anthropology Undergraduate Association Journal (University of California)
http://ucaua.org

Student Anthropologist (National Association of Student Anthropologists [USA])
http://studentanthropologist.wordpress.com/

The Unfamiliar: An Anthropological Journal (University of Edinburgh)
http://journals.ed.ac.uk/unfamiliar/

Janet celebrated after handing in her dissertation and then set about organizing a few follow-up activities. Her photographs had formed a key part of her research and analysis and she was keen to share these with a wider audience. She found a student art space at her university and compiled an exhibition on the bodily aesthetics of death and bereavement in Mexico, using a selection of her photographs, extracts from her fieldnotes and analytical discussion from her dissertation. She organized a small opening event and invited her flatmates, friends and family. It was a fun event and her images and arguments sparked a lot of lively discussion, but Janet felt the opinions of the undertakers and vernacular embalmers themselves were missing from all of this. What would they make of her work? So, she set up a website and created a digital Spanish version of the exhibition for her funerary informants, some of whom posted their own comments and reactions on the site. Janet also discovered an online network of anthropologists working on various aspects of the anthropology of death. She found it all so interesting and although she was still unsure what she would do after her degree, she began to think about developing her work into a larger, postgraduate research project.

The end of the writing up process had been very tough for **John**, but his brother was recovering well and life had settled down a bit. Now that the dissertation was finished he just wanted to relax for a while and enjoy some of the things he had missed while busily writing up. However, he had committed to providing the managers of the race track with a short research report and thought it would be easier to write this while the dissertation was still fresh in his mind. While reading over his work John remembered what had drawn him to this project in the first place and his interest in social policy issues. His fieldwork had made some new and original insights into the 'science' of greyhound-racing and the role of luck in gambling. The scholarly and policy literature on problem gambling made little or no mention of this important relationship. What was the point if his dissertation just stayed on the shelf? John decided to contact a gambling addiction charity he had spoken with during his research and began to transform some of his findings into a short policy brief for the organization. He was excited by the thought that in addition to its academic merits, his research might be useful in some way, and began to seek information about careers in which he might practise anthropology in an applied setting.

Skills and attributes

What have you learned, what skills have you acquired, and which attributes have you enhanced through doing your own research project? Designing, conducting and writing up an independent research project within a fixed time-frame is a significant achievement. Whatever kind of anthropology project you have done, you will have developed key generic skills in critical thinking and communication of information and argument. Taking a bit of time to reflect on the capabilities and competencies you have developed will allow you to showcase your intellectual, communicative and interpersonal skills for prospective employers or academic research councils.

The kinds of 'life skills' or 'graduate attributes' you will have acquired or enhanced through the research process are more general than the discipline-specific knowledge you have gained during your anthropology degree, and imply a diverse range of skills and personal qualities. Hager and Holland's (2010) list of possible 'graduate attributes' is a useful way to begin thinking about your own research process and the skills you have acquired or improved. Attributes, they suggest, include:

> thinking skills such as logical and analytical reasoning, problem solving and intellectual curiosity; effective communication skills, teamwork skills, and capacities to identify, access and manage knowledge and information; personal attributes such as imagination, creativity and intellectual rigor; and values, such as ethical practice, persistence, integrity and tolerance.
>
> (Hager and Holland 2010: 2–3).

Try to think about what you have learned, what you have achieved and what capacities you have developed in the process.

Some of the attributes and competencies you may have developed or enhanced through your anthropology research project are listed in the box below:

Box 9.2

Research and enquiry

- apply different theories to the interpretation and explanation of human conduct and patterns of behaviour;
- judge the value and relevance of empirical evidence and theoretical argument and interpretation in social science;
- identify and design ways of solving problems with a social and cultural dimension;
- interpret and analyze a variety of textual, oral and visual forms;

- discuss ideas and interpretations with others in a clear and reasoned way; and
- assess the ethical implications of anthropological research and enquiry.

Personal and intellectual autonomy

- be an independent learner who takes responsibility for their own learning and is committed to continuous reflection, self-evaluation and self-improvement;
- be able to make decisions on the basis of rigorous and independent thought, taking into account ethical and professional issues;
- be able to respond effectively to unfamiliar problems in unfamiliar contexts; and
- have a personal vision and goals and be able to work towards these in a sustainable way.

Communication

- learn new language skills and use them to communicate effectively with others;
- make effective use of oral, written and visual means to critique, negotiate, create and communicate understanding; and
- use communication as a tool for collaborating and relating to others.

Personal effectiveness

- be both adaptive and proactively responsive to changing social contexts;
- have the confidence to make decisions based on their understandings and their personal and intellectual autonomy; and
- transfer their knowledge, learning, skills and abilities from one context to another.

(selected extracts from *Social Anthropology Honours Programme Handbook 2012–13*)

Take a look at your university's resources to do with graduate attributes for additional information. There are plenty of useful resources available in which you can find out more about the recent focus on student skills and 'graduate attributes', keep up with developments in higher education, and get some useful tips for reflecting on your own capabilities and qualities.

Some useful resources:

The student experience section of The Guardian Higher Education Network (UK): http://www.guardian.co.uk/higher-education-network/student-experience. See

Mick Healey's article 'Rethinking the undergraduate dissertation' for an example: http://www.guardian.co.uk/higher-education-network/blog/2011/jun/28/flexible-dissertations-for-undergraduates?INTCMP=SRCH

The Quality Assurance Agency for Higher Education, Scotland (UK), Enhancement Themes website contains a series of resources and briefing papers. These are primarily aimed at academics and higher education professionals. See, for example: Gun, Vicky et al. 2008. 'Enhancing Graduate Attributes: Arts, Humanities and Social Sciences', http://www.enhancementthemes.ac.uk/docs/publications/enhancing-graduate-attributes-arts-humanities-and-social-sciences.pdf?sfvrsn=14

The Times Higher Education (UK), http://www.timeshighereducation.co.uk

The Chronicle of Higher Education (USA), http://chronicle.com

References

Hager, Paul and Susan Holland. 2010. *Graduate Attributes, Learning and Employability*. Dordrecht: Springer.

Social Anthropology Honours Programme Handbook 2012–13. Edinburgh: University of Edinburgh, http://www.sps.ed.ac.uk/__data/assets/word_doc/0006/70746/Social_Anthropology_Honours_Booklet_2012-13.doc.

Walliman, Nicholas. 2005. *Your Research Project: A Step-by-step Guide for the First-time Researcher*. 2nd edition. London: Sage.

Index

Abu-Lughod, Lila 130
access and permissions 16–17, 32–33,
   70–71, 96–97, 105; language 84;
   participant observation 77
anthropology 7–11; anthropology
   'at home' 9, 13–14, 96; and 'crisis of
   representation' 63, 118–19
Apache 135–37; *see also* Basso, Keith
audio and visual information 31, 40,
   50, 53

Balinese cockfight 133–35; *see also* Geertz,
   Clifford
Basso, Keith 135–37
Benedict, Ruth 39
Biehl, João 118
Boas, Franz 10
Bourdieu, Pierre 65–66
boxers 66, 82
Briggs, Jean 72–73, 76
budget 34

calendar; secondary research activities 47
CAQDAS (Computer Assisted Qualitative
   Data Analysis) 109–10; *see also* software
   tools
claims and evidence 132–35
Clifford, James and George Marcus 63
Comaroff, Jean and John 57
contingencies: 'Plan B' 72–74
Csordas, Thomas 65–67, 75, 76, 78

Danforth, Lorraine 15–16
data 104–6; data analysis 115–16; data
   management 48, 51, 52, 106–11;
   interpretation 111–15
dissemination 144; conference papers,
   posters, visual presentations 145;
   exhibitions and film screenings 145–46;

journal articles 146; reports and
   presentations 144–45
Dwyer, Kevin 63–65, 67, 76, 78

Edmonds, Alexander 16, 18, 71
elicitation 26
embodied experience 65–67
ethical issues 14, 28–30, 67, 78;
   anthropology and the military 93;
   identification of interlocutors 93;
   informed consent 28, 93–95; political
   agenda 92; professional guidelines 94;
   relations and responsibilities 94–95;
   responsibilities to interlocutors 92–93
ethics committees and review 28–30, 91–92
ethnographic research methods 24–28, 58,
   74–84; secondary research methods 37–54;
   and writing up 129–32
ethnography 9, 24, 38, 39, 41, 56, 57, 59,
   116
ethnology 40
evaluative criteria: secondary research 42
Evans-Pritchard, E. E. 8, 9, 56, 59,
   116
evidence: claims and producing a credible
   argument 120, 132–37; and mind
   mapping 123–25; secondary research 42

Farmer, Paul 92
field notes 71, 85–89, 99, 107–8; security
   88–89, 99
field site 16–17; and language 31,
   84–85; and where and how to live
   70–72
fieldwork 9, 13–14, 16–17, 37–39, 55–69,
   70–90; fieldwork *habitus* 86–88;
   secondary sources 53
focus groups 26, 108
free writing 122–25